Crossing Borders with Literature of Diversity

The Bill Harp Professional Teacher's Library

CROSSING BORDERS WITH LITERATURE OF DIVERSITY

by Julia Candace Corliss

Christopher-Gordon Publishers, Inc.
Norwood, Massachusetts

Credits

Every effort has been made to contact copyright holders for permission to reproduce borrowed material where necessary. We apologize for any oversights and would be happy to rectify them in future printings.

All student work used with permission.

Copyright © 1998 by Christopher-Gordon Publishers, Inc.

All rights reserved. Except for review purposes, no part of this material protected by this copyright notice may be reproduced or utilized in any form or by any means, electronic or mechanical, including photocopying, recording, or any information and retrieval system, without the express written permission of the publisher or copyright owner.

The Bill Harp Professional Teacher's Library
An Imprint of
Christopher-Gordon Publishers, Inc.
1502 Providence Highway, Suite #12
Norwood, MA 02062
(800) 934-8322

Printed in the United States of America

10 9 8 7 6 5 4 3 2 1   02 01 00 99 98

Library of Congress Catalog Card Number: 98-071293
ISBN: 0-926842-81-1

Dedication

This book is dedicated to all the fine authors, illustrators, and educators of literature of diversity who create such books that we might hold them in our hands, read them, and thereby become more adept at crossing borders.

"We have no borders when we read."

—Naomi Shihab Nye

Acknowledgments

Both professionally and personally, I have many people to thank for their guidance, inspiration, and support which have contributed so much toward bringing this book into being.

I would like to thank Dr. Doty Hale of Claremont Graduate University for her guidance and patience as she encouraged the growth of this work at its beginning. I especially thank Sue Canavan of Christopher-Gordon Publishers who shared my vision and helped me make that vision a reality. I am grateful to the reviewers and editing staff who worked with my manuscript and helped me see the work with "fresh eyes." I thank the staff of Mrs. Nelson's Toy & Book Shop who helped whenever I called. I am grateful to the administration and staff at The Mirman School who have shown support for literature of diversity all along the way. I am very appreciative of the support and participation of the students and families of The Mirman School who have read, discussed, and worked with this literature every step of the way with me.

I thank my parents, John and Margarette Lawson, who first taught me about crossing borders. I would also like to thank my husband, Burt Corliss, for his unflagging support and encouragement. I would like to thank Kortyana, James Jr., Javonne, and Latreia Williams, my great nieces and nephews, whose love fueled my writing. I hope the books highlighted here will one day be in their classrooms.

Contents

Preface ix

SECTION I

Chapter 1 Introduction 1
    The Theme: Crossing Borders 1
    Purpose 2
    Rationale 3
    Definitions in the Professional Literature 4
    Definitions in This Book 5
    Terms Used for Identification of Cultural/Ethnic Groups 5
    How This Book Is Structured 6

Chapter 2 A Brief History of Children's Book Publishing
of Literature of Diversity in the United States Since 1960 7

SECTION II

Chapter 3 Physical Borders 9
    Crossing Borders Within a City or Country 10
    Crossing Global Borders 17

Chapter 4 Cultural Borders 25
    History 25
    Biography/Autobiography 31

viii *Crossing Borders With Literature of Diversity*

    Poetry and Short Stories 39
    Folklore Anthologies 47

Chapter 5   Inner Borders **51**
    Friends and Families 51
    Courage and Survival 57
    War and Peace 60
    Perspectives on Prejudice 62

SECTION III

Chapter 6   Using Literature of Diversity in the Classroom **65**
    Individualized Reading 65
    Thematic Units 74
    Literature Circles 79
    Challenges 85

Chapter 7   Selecting Literature of Diversity **87**
    Literary Quality 87
    Authenticity 87
    Bias 88
    Balance 88
    Selection Tips for Teachers 89
    General Selection Questions 89
    Specific Method and Selection Criteria for This Book 91
    Focus Questions Guiding Title Selection for This Book 92
    Final Thoughts on Selection of Literature of Diversity 92

Afterword   Teacher to Teacher **93**

Appendix A   Thematic Groupings **95**

Appendix B   Cultural/Ethnic Groupings **99**

Appendix C   Literary Genre Groupings **105**

References **109**

Author Index **111**

Subject Index **113**

Preface

I am a classroom teacher. I am a reader and a poet. I love literature and children. My classroom is crammed with books. The best pieces of classroom furniture I have are bookcases. A few years ago, while doing graduate work at Claremont Graduate University, I took a critical look at my classroom library collection. I realized with a jolt that it did not reflect cultural diversity to the degree that it should. There were some excellent titles of diversity such as *Dragonwings* by Laurence Yep, *Baseball in April* by Gary Soto, *Roll of Thunder Hear My Cry* by Mildred Taylor, *If the People Could Fly* by Virginia Hamilton, and *The Hundred Penny Box* by Sharon Bell Mathis, as well as the poetry of Gary Soto, Eloise Greenfield, Maya Angelou, and Langston Hughes, but I knew that wasn't enough. There weren't enough books and there wasn't enough diversity. At that time my collection was mostly a reflection of the Euro-American dominated contemporary publishing scene of children's literature and my own Euro-American upbringing and culture. I decided to change what I saw by adding to my classroom library collection. I was teaching fourth grade, and I could best afford purchases in paperback. I needed to know more about literature of diversity. So, I immersed myself in reading titles reflecting the kaleidoscope of human diversity that were available in paperback and were appropriate for a fourth through sixth grade classroom. At the same time, as a part of my graduate work, I read the professional literature pertaining to the publication and use of literature of diversity in schools. Thus, this book reflects my reading, thinking, and practice in the classroom. It is also a result of my personal commitment to growth and change. My classroom library now houses most of the books highlighted in this book. It has taken years to read and acquire them.

As I read the books you will read about here, my worldview was expanding. I was learning more about crossing borders of time, space, culture, experience, and thought by reading and reflecting on these books, as well as studying the work of researchers who were writing about diversity in education. I kept reading. Book by book, using the scalpels of honesty and reflection, I learned to recognize the difference between books written from an insider's perspective and those written from an outsider's perspective. As I read the fine works you will find highlighted in the "Borders" chapters of this book, I cried and laughed and pondered and celebrated and delved deeper. My sensitivities and sensibilities toward the diversity of human cultures I met in these books deepened. I attempted to attune myself to nuances of language and stretch my consciousness to walk in shoes that did not belong to me.

Always, throughout these years of reading, reflecting, and studying, I returned to my classroom with these books. Because discussion enhances understanding for me, I shared the books with my students, and I talked with my students about them. I listened with my heart and my head to what they said. I talked with other teachers about the books and I saw that other teachers hungered to know more about these books too. So, the idea for *Crossing Borders* was born.

I am an outsider of every culture represented in the books in this collection, except the Euro-American culture into which I was born. However, reading these books has helped me to understand more about crossing borders that have been imposed by culture, time, space, and thought. I believe that most people, regardless of their cultural backgrounds, are more familiar with their own cultures than with others. Such cultural ethnocentricity changes only when people make an effort to educate themselves in some way about cultures into which they were not born. None of us can unzip our skins and step into someone else's, nor can most of us travel extensively and immerse ourselves in other cultures as a means of bringing about understanding of the nuances of those other cultures. However, regardless of our own sociocultural background, and assuming that we are literate, what we can do is read beyond the borders of our own backgrounds, discuss our reading, and begin to increase our knowledge of others through engaging with the body of authentic literature of diversity that is available. Then, in our role as teachers, we can bring this literature of diversity into our classrooms. Reading and responding to this literature will enrich both ourselves and our students.

I see the image of crossing borders as a metaphor for change leading to growth. Change can be frightening, exciting, exhilarating, and rewarding. It is often difficult. When we allow ourselves to be limited by our physical, cultural, and inner borders, the scope of who we are and who we can be individually and collectively is severely restricted. Such limitations mean that we surrender our power to learn and grow beyond the borders of our birth culture. Literature of diversity provides us with a tool for change. I am not so naive that I think that reading, reflecting upon, and talking about these books alone will eradicate divisions in our society based on ethnicity, gender, class, religion, culture, or power. However, I do think that reading and responding to these books is a place to start effecting a change of thought and awareness which has the potential to move us toward a fuller understanding and appreciation of one another.

Moreover, literature of diversity offers us a tangible weapon to fight xenophobia, or fear of strangers. Xenophobia is a dangerous thing. It ultimately can lead to prejudice, hatred, war, concentration camps, and genocide. By reading and discussing this literature with our students and each other, we can facilitate for ourselves and our students the broadening of our worldviews and come to know each other not as strangers, but as fellow human beings who share this planet Earth, our home.

As teachers, the complexities of borders of ethnicity, culture, religion, class, gender, and power face us every day as we seek to understand our students so that we may improve in our ability to teach them. I believe that literature is a powerful tool that can help us and our students cross borders that separate us so that understanding and respect may flourish in our classrooms as a foundation upon which to build learning. This book is humbly presented with the hope that it will help contribute to the development of a much needed equitable literature curriculum in schools.

Thus, I invite you to join me on this journey of crossing borders with literature of diversity. Thankfully, as long as fine writers—such as those you will meet in this book—keep writing and publishing, there will be many good books to help us cross new borders and continue to grow.

COME AND READ WITH ME

Come and read with me
Cross borders of time and space
Travel to places you've never been
Meet people you've never seen
Come and read with me.

Traverse these pages
And find pain and joy
Mirrored within
Know struggle and heartache
And taste victory so sweet.

Come and read with me
Sing of the beauty of the human spirit
Persevering, questing,
Rising to meet life's challenges
In all its complexities.

Come and read with me
Laugh at childhood antics
And innocent moments sublime
Cringe with shame and swell with pride
Feel your heartbeat race
Delve into the hearts of others
And know your own better.

Come and read with me
Open yourself to change
Open yourself to growth
Open yourself to all to be found
Within these pages
Come and read with me.

SECTION I
CHAPTER 1

Introduction

The Theme: Crossing Borders

We live in a culturally diverse, pluralistic world. Our world contains not only political and cultural borders between countries, but is made more complex by having cultural borders of class, ethnicity, gender, religion, language, and so on within countries. At the same time, human beings are interconnected by universal human concerns, such as family, love, work, fears, wishes, dreams, ambitions, and hopes. We are one species, *Homo sapiens,* and yet the cultural diversity within our species, combined with the pluralistic nature of our society and world, means that in one way or another, we are all border crossers.

Crossing Physical Borders

Sometimes we are border crossers because we cross a physical border, moving from one place to another, thereby adding to our life experience. This movement across physical borders helps to shape who we are and how we fit into the world, as well as how we see the world. Through literature, we can share the experience of such physical crossings without transporting our bodies.

Crossing Cultural Borders

In this age of global technology, international business, and cultural pluralism, there are also cultural borders for all of us to cross. Every culture has its storytellers and poets. Every culture has its heroes/heroines and history, the people and events of that culture which make it unique.

Through literature we can come to know the stories, poetry, and history of a culture. Thus, literature is an appropriate vehicle for helping us to expand our worldview through coming to know more about each other. Such cultural knowledge gained through literature has the potential to facilitate border crossings when they occur in life.

Crossing Inner Borders

Finally, we all have inner borders that demarcate the negative and positive parts of who we are. The balance between these positive and negative factors differs for everyone, and is connected to the totality of each individual's life experience. For instance, such negative factors as prejudice and fear can prevent us from understanding and appreciating the life experiences and cultures of others. Conversely, such positive factors as courage and respect for others can lead us to greater understanding and appreciation of others. The negative and positive aspects of ourselves are reflected in our attitudes, thoughts, words, and deeds. The negative parts of ourselves can impede our personal growth in such areas as awareness, compassion, tolerance, and understanding. Moreover, negative attitudes, thoughts, words, and behavior can affect how we feel about ourselves, which in turn can affect how we behave toward others. Our inner borders can keep us entrenched in our own negativity and thus growth of spirit, heart, and mind is lessened. Literature educates the heart as well as the mind. Literature can be a bridge to help us grow beyond the confines of our own particular lived cultural experience. Literature can help us cross our inner borders, and thereby expand our understanding and appreciation of others and ourselves.

Purpose

Although we live in a pluralistic society, cultural pluralism is often not reflected in the literature used in elementary literacy education. There is a great need for the development of an equitable literature curriculum in our schools. In 1992, Applebee showed that there is a limited amount of literature reflecting diversity being used regularly as part of the core literature curriculum in both private and public schools in the United States. All students in our classrooms need to feel included in the process of literacy education, which includes reading, writing, speaking, and listening. The literature which is read, discussed, and written about by students is a key aspect of their literacy development, and the particular literature that students and teachers read and respond to influences their sense of self and their worldview. The development of an equitable literature curriculum across cultures will enhance the self-esteem of readers previously not reflected in children's literature used in the classroom and hopefully enlighten those who have only seen themselves in the children's literature they read (Howard, 1991). Therefore, an equitable literature curriculum is needed to expand how students see themselves, others, and the world around them (Bishop, 1987; Bishop, 1997). It is the purpose of this book to be a practical tool for all those who work with children ages eight to twelve, and who wish to make an equitable literature curriculum part of the school-centered reading experiences of the children with whom they work, as well as introduce literature of diversity into their own reading.

This book is especially meant to provide a user-friendly resource for teachers that will help them increase their knowledge and expand their use of culturally diverse literature in their classrooms. Although this book is targeted to upper elementary teachers and students (fourth–sixth grades), it may also be useful to teachers and students in grade levels above and below the fourth through sixth grades. Teacher educators in colleges and universities may also find this book useful in acquainting both preservice and inservice teachers with literature that reflects diverse cultures, perspectives, and sensibilities. Parents and librarians may also may find this book a useful resource for expanding their knowledge of literature of diversity targeted for eight- to twelve-year-olds. The titles included in the annotation sections of this book are available in paperback. Although there are more fine titles of diversity available, other than those that appear in paperback, it is the purpose of this book to assist in making titles reflecting diversity more accessible to educators, parents, and students. It is hoped that the affordability of paperbacks will increase the opportunity for literature of diversity to actually be read by students and teachers.

Rationale

Literature has an important role to play in our pluralistic society, because it can develop and extend understandings related to living in such a diverse society. Literature shows us our common humanity, how we are connected through our emotions, needs, and desires. "Understanding our common humanity is a powerful weapon against the forces that would divide and alienate us from one another" (Bishop, 1987, p. 60). Literature also helps us to understand and appreciate the differences among us. Literature for young people plays a strong role in the transmission of values, as well as aiding in the development of "an understanding of the effects of social issues and forces on the lives of ordinary individuals" (Bishop, 1987, p. 60). Inclusion of literature of diversity in the curriculum is important then for increasing cultural awareness and thereby expanding the worldviews of students.

Children need to feel good about who they are in order to fully participate in a classroom setting. Self-esteem for children of color is about perceptions and freedom to be themselves (Henderson, 1991). In order to develop strong self-esteem, it is important that children receive positive messages about themselves. Literature of diversity is a strong ally in providing those positive messages for children. Institutional racism exists, and "racism cuts at the very heart and very sense of self in the developing child of color" (Henderson, 1991, p. 21). Literature of diversity is important because it says to children of color that others (people who write, illustrate, and publish books, as well as teachers who present those books) think they are important enough to be in books. This growing body of literature is a quiet weapon against institutional racism (Henderson, 1991). When the life experiences of children of color are mirrored in books, they and their cultures are affirmed. However, when children are excluded or denigrated in literature, they receive a very different kind of message. "They learn that they are not valued members of society and that reading can be a negative or hurtful experience" (Bishop, 1987, p. 61). Such a negative message is counterproductive to the development of literacy and fully participating children who feel good about themselves.

Thus, through reading literature that reflects diversity, students have the opportunity to see themselves and have their cultures and realities affirmed through print, as well as see the cultures and realities of others unlike themselves and thereby expand their views of others. Using literature of diversity in the classroom reading/language arts program is a way of empowering students through enhancing their sense of self and expanding their ability to value the life experiences and histories of others different from themselves (Bishop, 1987; De La Luz Reyes, et al., 1993; Harris, 1994; Johnson & Smith, 1993; Tway, 1989; Yokota, 1994).

Definitions in the Professional Literature

Generally, literature that reflects diversity has been known as multicultural literature. There is general agreement that such literature is about persons or groups that differ in some way (ethnically, racially, culturally, linguistically, sexual orientation, or disabilities) from the sociopolitical Euro-American mainstream of the United States (Bishop, 1992; Cai & Bishop, 1994; Bishop, 1997). Thus, there is consensus that this body of literature includes works by and about people of color both inside the United States and globally (Bishop, 1992; Howard, 1991; Kruse, 1992; Bishop, 1997). However, there is less agreement about the inclusion of nonmainstream Euro-American ethnic groups, such as Jewish, Amish, and residents of Appalachia (Bishop, 1992).

Some writers have taken a more inclusive approach to defining literature of diversity. Using the term multicultural literature, Yokota (1993) placed emphasis on the "multi" part of the term *multicultural* and defined multicultural literature as "literature that represents any distinct cultural group through accurate portrayal and rich detail" (p. 157). Johnson and Smith (1993) considered multicultural literature to be those works that helped students explore issues of diversity connected to gender, age or generation, family structure, ethnicity, race, and culture. Themes embedded within this literature included prejudice and discrimination, families, friendship/peer pressure, and self-awareness. Johnson and Smith (1993) identified literature that reflected a diversity of experiences and included works that depicted distinct Euro-American cultural groups, such as Jewish Americans. The term multiethnic literature has begun to appear in the professional literature in place of multicultural (Reimer, 1992; Harris, 1997). "Multicultural literature should be defined in a comprehensive and inclusive manner; that is, it should include books that reflect the racial, ethnic, and social diversity that is characteristic of our pluralistic society and of the world" (Bishop, 1997, p. 3).

Definitions in This Book

The previous discussion of definitions suggests that to create a truly equitable literature curriculum, a culturally inclusive definition of this literature is necessary. Toward that end, in this book, the term *multicultural literature* will be replaced with the term *literature of diversity*. Literature of diversity is literature that reflects the broad range of human experience and a global kaleidoscope of cultures. It is meant to reflect the pluralistic world in which we live. However, because it is recognized that there is a limited amount of literature by and about people of color being used in classrooms (Anaya, 1992; Applebee, 1992; Harris, 1994; Jay, 1991; Reimer, 1992; Powell, 1992), emphasis has been placed on identifying a body of literature by and about people of color in order to contribute to the development of an equitable literature curriculum. In addition, this book also includes European or Euro-American works when those works add to the kaleidoscope of human experience and connect to an aspect of the overall theme of crossing borders. Therefore, the term *literature of diversity* will be used to encompass the broadest possible range of human experience as revealed through this literature.

Terms Used for Identification of Cultural/Ethnic Groups

The terms used for identification of cultural/ethnic groups are meant to be descriptive and specific. Therefore, with respect to groups outside the

United States, books are identified using the term for the country of the main character of a work of fiction or topic in nonfiction. With respect to cultural/ethnic groups within the United States, the term is used which indicates the continent or country of origin of familial ancestors of the main character or topic (nonfiction) in combination with American (e.g., African American, Japanese American, Euro-American). The exceptions to this usage occur in the cases of Native Americans and Hispanic Americans. In much of the literature, Native Americans are referred to equally as Native American, Indian, and American Indian without stigma (Slapin, Seale, 1992; Stensland, 1979; Bishop, 1994). Therefore, although most of the time the term *Native American* is used, there are times when the other two terms are also used. With respect to Hispanic Americans, whenever possible the most specific identification possible is used, such as Mexican American. The general terms *Hispanic American* and *Latino/a* are used interchangeably. These choices concerning cultural/ethnic identification terminology were guided by the desire to use positive, descriptive, specific terminology that would authentically describe the cultural/ethnic variation of people across the broad spectrum of humanity reflected in the works cited in the annotation sections of this book. No group has been intentionally excluded. If particular titles of quality, authentic literature available in paperback do not appear here, I invite my readers to tell me about those books. I am always open to learning about books that will enhance the development of my students and myself as border crossers.

How This Book Is Structured

This book is divided into four sections. Section I includes Chapters 1 and 2. Chapter 1 presents a discussion of this book's theme, purpose, rationale, and definitions of terms. Chapter 2 discusses the publishing of children's books reflecting diversity since 1960. Section II is the annotations section. It includes Chapters 3, 4, and 5 where the books are grouped thematically according to the "Crossing Borders" theme of this book: Chapter 3 deals with physical borders, Chapter 4 with cultural borders, and Chapter 5 with inner borders. Section III includes Chapters 6 and 7. Chapter 6 focuses on the practical use of literature of diversity as part of the reading/language arts curriculum throughout the year in the classroom. Chapter 7 deals with issues involved with selecting literature of diversity. The fourth section, the appendixes, offers alternative ways of thinking about grouping the titles highlighted in Section II to aid in curriculum planning. Also included is an appendix of possible sources for purchasing the books.

Chapter 2

A Brief History of Children's Book Publishing of Literature of Diversity in the United States Since 1960

The emergence of literature written and/or illustrated by people of color in children's book publishing in the United States in the second half of the twentieth century is closely tied to the development of multicultural education as it grew out of the Civil Rights Movement in the 1960s (Bishop, 1997). Therefore, African Americans were the first nonmainstream group to be recognized as being underrepresented in the world of children's books. Larrick (1965) surveyed publishers of children's books to determine the degree to which African Americans were represented in 5000 children's books published between 1962 and 1964. Her work showed that the number of books including African Americans published during those years was 349, or an average of 6.7 percent. The authenticity of that small percentage was also poor. First, almost 60 percent of those 349 books dealt with Negroes from countries outside the United States or with American Negroes before World War II. (*Negro* was the identification term of respect used by Larrick in this 1965 article.) The use of stereotypes was rampant. Most of the books had been written by Euro-American authors.

In the mid-1960s, the Council for Interracial Books for Children (CIBC) was formed to encourage authors and artists of color to create books for children (Horning & Kruse, 1991). One of the ways the council accomplished its goal was through contests for unpublished writers and illustrators of color. Winners received a cash prize and an all-important connection to the world of children's book publishing. The winners of the CIBC's contests from 1967 to 1979 include many contemporary authors of color such as Sharon Bell Mathis, Walter Dean Myers, Mildred D. Taylor, Virginia Driving Hawk Sneve, and Ai-Ling Louie. CIBC also showcased illustrators of color, including some of today's well-known artists such as

Donald Crews, Pat Cummings, and Leo Dillon. The CIBC continued to function and promote authors and illustrators of color until it went out of existence in 1993 after the death of Brad Chambers, an influential founder (Ford, 1994).

Throughout the late 1960s and early 1970s the publishing industry expanded the publishing of literature of diversity for children and young adults. This increase to some extent reflected dawning recognition of the diversity of an increasingly pluralistic society, as well as the social consciousness aroused by the U.S. Civil Rights Movement (Horning & Kruse, 1991). More influential, however, was the recognition by the publishing industry that there was increased consumer demand for such works (Horning & Kruse, 1991; Ford, 1994). During the decade of the 1970s, the percentages of African American representation doubled, with 14.4 percent of children's books from this period having African Americans included in text or illustrations (Yokota, 1993). The works of many fine authors and illustrators of color were launched during this period, including those of Lucille Clifton, Alice Childress, Tom Feelings, Eloise Greenfield, Rosa Guy, Julius Lester, Nicholasa Mohr, Jerry Pinkney, John Steptoe, and Laurence Yep. Yokota (1993) reports that during the 1980s what data is available suggests a return to a low percentage of newly published books reflecting diversity.

During the 1990s there has been a renewed commitment to publishing literature of diversity, which the publishing industry has come to define in market terms as books by and about people of color (Horning & Kruse, 1991). Ford (1994) identified two current markets for this literature. One market is culturally focused and consists of the group of people that any particular book reflects, so that the children of that group can see themselves in a book. These culturally focused groups tend to purchase books that reflect their own culture. The other market consists of people across cultures who want children to know about the diversity of people and cultures through print. Small publishing houses have come into being in response to these two markets. Three such companies are Lee & Low Books, Just Us Books, and Arte de Publico Press.

As larger mainstream publishing companies respond to these market needs, providing editorial support becomes an issue. Although the number of literature of diversity book projects continues to grow, "the ethnic diversity of editors has not increased proportionately" (Ford, 1994, p. 33). The publishing world of children's books is predominantly Euro-American and middle class. Unless such editors make an effort to immerse themselves in the reading of authentic literature of diversity, they may pass over good work for a variety of culturally embedded reasons (Ford, 1994). There is a need for editors of color in the world of children's literature publishing to help provide a more culturally balanced perspective. Hopefully, the commitment to publishing quality works of children's literature by and about people of color will continue throughout the years ahead.

SECTION II
CHAPTER 3

Physical Borders

This collection of literature of diversity includes works of fiction, poetry, folklore, and nonfiction (including biography). Most of the fiction in paperback available for review was contemporary realistic fiction and historical fiction. There was only a limited number of high literary quality works of fantasy written by or about people of color.

Therefore, the novel-length works of fiction included in this collection are contemporary realistic fiction and historical fiction. However, works of folklore and short stories that sometimes had a fantasy element were also included. Perhaps in the future there will be more novel-length works of fantasy for upper elementary students written by and about people of color from which to choose. There is a definite need for works of this type.

The bibliographical information about the titles in the entries included in the chapters in this section was obtained directly from the books. Three broad reading levels (RL) were noted: Easy (E), Medium (M), and Difficult (D). These broad reading levels were determined by taking into account vocabulary, syntax, content, and length of the book. These reading levels are meant to be general guidelines only. Length of the book was considered, because this often matters to fourth- through sixth-grade students. The titles in each of the chapters in Section II are grouped in subcategories delineated at the beginning of each chapter to add to the ease of using this resource.

The works cited in this section generally include two genres of fiction: (1) contemporary realistic fiction and (2) historical fiction. When the time in which a story was set was fifty or more years earlier than the present, it was categorized as historical fiction. The stories in both fiction genres had characters who moved across one or more physical borders that delineated countries or states, or crossed borders within a city where movement was from one neighborhood to another.

Therefore, the subcategories within this chapter are: (1) Crossing Borders Within a City or Country and (2) Crossing Global Borders. In these stories, movement across physical borders brought about changes in the characters' lives. Often the characters in these stories found themselves in a new environment where they had to build a new life for themselves. Frequently, the journeys undertaken by the characters within these stories were filled with challenges.

Crossing Borders Within a City or Country

Armstrong, Jennifer. (1992). *Steal Away . . . to Freedom*. New York: Orchard Books. (HB). New York: Scholastic, Inc., 1993. (PB). Novel. Historical Fiction. African American. Euro-American. 207 pp. ISBN 0-590-46921-5. RL=M

The story begins in 1896 when Euro-American Susannah, now a grandmother, receives a letter from her African American friend Bethlehem who is very ill in Toronto, Canada, and wants to see her. Bethlehem wants to record the story of their escape from Virginia during slavery times. So, Susannah takes her granddaughter Mary to Toronto where they meet Bethlehem and her young caretaker Free. Mary and Free struggle to know one another as they act as scribes while Susannah and Bethlehem tell the story of their combined escape from the South to the North in 1855. For Susannah that journey meant coming back to Vermont and for Bethlehem that journey meant freedom and a new life in Canada. After Susannah's parents died, she went to live in Virginia with her uncle. He gave her a slave, Bethlehem, a young girl of about the same age. Bethlehem and Susannah became friends and eventually they ran away together. The book alternates chapters set in 1896 with chapters set in 1855 as Susannah and Bethlehem tell the story of their friendship and their journey. The cover on the paperback edition depicts two girls in modern hiking clothing and should be ignored, because the story itself is authentic to the period.

Conlon-McKenna, Marita. (1990). *Under the Hawthorn Tree*. Ireland: O'Brien Press Ltd. (HB). New York: Puffin Books, 1992. (PB). Novel. Historical Fiction. Irish. 122 pp. ISBN 0-14-036031-X. RL=M

The Great Famine of 1845–1850 has struck Ireland. The potato is the crop of the poor people, and a strange blight has destroyed the potatoes all over Ireland. People are starving. There is very little work. Eily, Michael, Peggy, and the baby Bridget live with their father and mother, John and Margaret O'Driscoll. Their father leaves to find work and doesn't return. The baby Bridget dies and is buried under the hawthorn tree, and then their mother leaves to find their father and doesn't return. When the landlord's agent threatens to separate the children and put them in the workhouse, they decide to walk across Ireland to Castletaggart, hoping to find their great-aunts. They make the arduous and dangerous journey, managing to stay alive, and finally arrive in Castletaggart, where they find their two elderly aunts, who welcome them into their humble home. The author includes a brief history of the Great Famine at the end of the book to set the story of the O'Driscoll family in a historical context.

De Trevino, Elizabeth Borton. (1989). *El Guero: A True Adventure Story*. Illustrated by Leslie W. Bowman. Canada: HarperCollinsCanadaLtd. (HB). New York: Farrar Straus Giroux, A Sunburst Book, 1996. (PB) Novel. Historical Fiction. Fictionalized Biography. Mexican. 102 pp. ISBN 0-374-42028-9. RL=M

The author explains that the Guero of this story is her father-in-law Porfirio Trevino Arreola, who recounts to her the story of his adventures when the politics of Mexico cause a life change for his family. First, his family makes a hard journey from Mexico City to Ensenada. Then, due to the tyrannical hold and greed of a Mexican military man, Guero's father is imprisoned in Ensenada and the survival of the family is threatened unless a higher authority can be contacted. Guero overcomes his fears and, with the help of a friend, he escapes and makes his way to La Paz for help. He travels at first on the boat of Capt. Forker, an ally, until a storm renders the boat unseaworthy. Then, Guero continues on foot to La Paz, where he gains help in righting the situation.

Fenner, Carol. (1995). *Yolanda's Genius*. New York: Simon & Schuster Children's Publishing Division. (HB). New York: Scholastic Inc., 1996. (PB). Novel. Contemporary Realistic Fiction. African American Newbery Honor Book. 211 pp. ISBN 0-590-98859-X. RL=M

Fifth grader Yolanda Blue, her six-year-old brother Andrew, and their mother move away from Yolanda's beloved Chicago to Grand River, Michigan, because her mother hopes to provide them with a safer, healthier place to live and go to school than Chicago with its crime and drugs. However, drugs are a problem in Grand River also. Yolanda struggles in the new town to make friends and find a place for herself while helping take care of Andrew. One day, however, she neglects to bring Andrew home after school and the consequences are far reaching. His harmonica is destroyed by the leader of the Junior High druggie bad boys gang. Yolanda swears to protect Andrew and help him get his music back. Their Aunt Tiny comes to visit from Chicago and then takes all of them with her to Chicago for a visit. While there, Yolanda stumbles onto the Chicago Blues Festival and schemes to get Andrew an opportunity to play for the musicians. It works and the book ends with a stupendous scene featuring little Andrew Blue playing his own improvised composition in front of the Chicago Blues Festival at the behest of B.B. King, who shows a personal interest in Andrew Blue, musical prodigy.

Fleischman, Paul. (1993). *Bull Run*. Illustrated by David Frampton. New York: HarperCollins Children's Books. (HB). New York: HarperTrophy, a division of HarperCollins Publishers, 1995. (PB). Novel. Historical Fiction. Euro-American and African American. Scott O'Dell Award. 104 pp. ISBN 0-06-440588-5. RL=M

The setting of this novel is the battle of Bull Run, the first major battle of the American Civil War (1861–1865). The sixteen characters share their diverse perspectives—(Euro-American, African American, Northern and Southern, male and female)—on events, thoughts, and movements of people connected to Bull Run. Each chapter is expressed in the voice of a different character, and each character speaks more than once. Thus, there is constant shifting of point of view, which adds to the energy and breadth of this work. This novel could easily be transformed into a readers' theatre script for the classroom.

Hamilton, Virginia. (1968). *The House of Dies Drear.* New York: Macmillan Publishing Company. (HB). New York: The Trumpet Club, a division of Bantam Doubleday Dell Publishing Group, 1993. (PB). Novel. Combines Historical Fiction and Contemporary Realistic Fiction. African American. 280 pp. ISBN 0-440-84696-X. RL=D

Thomas Small, his mother, and his history professor father move to Ohio and into their newly purchased home, Drear House, which had been a way station on the Underground Railroad during Civil War times. In addition to its history, the house comes equipped with a legend that says it is haunted by two slave ghosts and the ghost of Dies Drear, the original builder and owner of the house. Thomas struggles to make a life for himself in his new home, which is like nothing he has ever known before. Besides the movement into the new house at the beginning of the story, there is a great deal of movement across borders separating the past and the present that occurs as Thomas explores Drear House and becomes more knowledgeable about its secrets. The ending is filled with drama and surprise as the legend, the mystery, and the present collide. *The Mystery of Drear House* (ISBN 0-02-043480-4) is a masterful and gripping sequel in which the author continues and concludes the story.

Houston, James. (1992). *Drifting Snow: An Arctic Search*. New York: Margaret K. McElderry Books, an imprint of Macmillan Publishing Co. (HB). New York: Puffin Books, 1994. (PB). Novel. Contemporary Realistic Fiction. Native American/Eskimo. 150 pp. ISBN 0-14-036530-3. RL=M

As a young child, Elizabeth is taken from her Inuit Eskimo parents, because she needs treatment for tuberculosis. She stays in the hospital for three years and then in a boarding school for seven years. Her identification tag and papers are lost. She is given a new name by someone in the Indian school. At the age of thirteen or fourteen, Elizabeth Queen returns to the Arctic to find her family, and to find out about herself and her people. She lives with an Inuit family, the Kiawak family, and learns about Inuit life through becoming involved in their ways and their struggle to survive in the Arctic. Eventually, they help her find her mother, father, and grandmother. In the end, Elizabeth and her grandmother choose to return with the Kiawaks to their nomadic life on Nesak Island to live close to the old ways of their ancestors.

Mohr, Nicholasa. (1979). *Felita*. Illustrated by Ray Cruz. New York: Dial Books. (HB). New York: A Bantam Skylark Book, 1990. (PB). Novel. Contemporary Realistic Fiction. Puerto Ricans. ISBN 0-553-15792-2. RL=M

Felita Maldonado, her two brothers Tito and Johnny, and their Mami and Papi move from their old neighborhood, which is filled with many friends, to a new neighborhood that Papi hopes will give them a better future. But, Felita's first day in the new neighborhood is filled with pain and fear, because she is taunted and attacked by other children with the sanction of their parents, who themselves are prejudiced against people who have a different skin color. Prejudice is powerfully portrayed in this story as each family member, including Mami, has an experience born of the racial prejudice in their new neighborhood. In the middle of the book, they return to their old neighborhood. Felita's *abuelita* (grandmother) gives them a welcome home dinner and when Felita spends the night, she gives Felita advice about how to think about her recent experiences with prejudice. Felita is glad to be reunited with her best friend Gigi, but then comes the Thanksgiving play at school, which causes tension between them. Once again, with Abuelita's wisdom to guide her, Felita makes up with her friend. Toward the end of the story, Abuelita becomes ill and dies, but the story ends with Felita talking with her uncle about taking a trip to Puerto Rico just as she and Abuelita had planned.

The sequel to this book is entitled *Going Home* (1989) and is also available in paperback (ISBN 0-553-15699-3). In the sequel, Felita journeys to Puerto Rico to spend the summer with her uncle. Again combatting prejudice, she comes to know her ancestral home in all its complexity.

Naidoo, Beverly. (1985). *Journey to Jo'burg: A South African Story.* England: Longman Group Limited. (HB). New York: Scholastic, Inc., 1986. (PB). Novella. Contemporary Realistic Fiction. South African. 80 pp. ISBN 0-06-440237-1. RL=E

Naledi and her little brother Tiro are very worried about their little sister Dineo, who is very ill. So, they walk 300 kilometers to Johannesburg to find their mother, so she can help them get medical assistance for Dineo, because there is no medical help available in the country town where they live. This story takes place in South Africa under apartheid. The prejudice and danger faced by black South Africans living in those times is shown through what happens to the children Naledi and Tiro as they cross the physical borders separating their black country home from the white part of Johannesburg where their mother works.

Porter, Connie. (1993). *Meet Addy, an American Girl. Book One.* Illustrations by Melodye Rosales. Middleton, WI: Pleasant Company Publications Incorporated. (HB). New York: Scholastic, Inc., 1994. (PB). Novella. Historical Fiction. African American. The American Girls Collection. 75 pp. ISBN 0-590-48329-3. RL=E

Shortly after Addy's Poppa is sold off the Southern plantation where they live, Addy and Momma make their escape to freedom. The way is difficult and scary, but they eventually make it to an Underground Railroad safe house and thence to safety and freedom. There are two other titles in this series that continue the story of Addy and her family: *Addy Learns a Lesson: A School Story* (ISBN 0-590-48330-7) and *Addy's Surprise* (ISBN 0-590-483331-5).

Price, Joan. (1982). *Truth Is a Bright Star.* Berkeley, California: Celestial Arts. (PB). Novel. Historical Fiction. Native American. 150 pp. ISBN 0-89087-333-X. RL=M

In 1832, Spanish soldiers kidnapped fourteen Hopi children and the young wife of Wickvaya, a Hopi youth, from the Hopi village of Oraibi on Third Mesa. The Spaniards sold their captives in Santa Fe as slaves. Wickvaya traveled the five hundred miles to Santa Fe and demanded a hearing with the governor. When the governor learned that the captives were Hopi, not the Spaniards' avowed enemies the Navajo, he ordered all the children and Wickvaya's wife to be returned. Mountain men who were not Spanish were also known to be present in the mountains around Santa Fe at this time in history.

This story of Loma, one of the captured Hopi children, who is purchased by a Euro-American mountain man named Big Jim, is based on these historical facts. The story is rich in cultural details brought out in the context of the story. Culture clash between Loma and Big Jim occurs when Big Jim seeks to train Loma to be his assistant in trapping beaver. However, throughout the story, Loma remains true to himself and his upbringing. Honoring all life forms is deeply embedded in his Hopi culture, so Loma is repulsed by the beaver trapping and killing for fur, and in fact at one point rescues a wounded beaver from one of Big Jim's traps, nurses it back to health, and releases it back into the wild when Big Jim leaves him alone at the camp. When Big Jim doesn't return, Loma does not run away, but instead searches for him with the help of Tall Walking Rain, a Taos shaman traveling from Santa Fe. They find an injured Big Jim and transport him back to the cabin, where Tall Walking Rain treats his injuries. A couple of weeks later, the arrival of Big Jim's friend and fellow mountain man Beaver Charlie is another pivotal point in the story. Beaver Charlie convinces Big Jim that he must return Loma to Santa Fe, because the governor is now aware the children are Hopi and not Navajo. In fact, in the end, Loma is returned safely to his family.

Soto, Gary. (1993). *The Pool Party.* Illustrated by Robert Casilla. New York: Delacorte Press. (HB). New York: Bantam Doubleday Dell Books for Young Readers, a division of Bantam Doubleday Dell Publishing Group, Inc., 1995. (PB). Novel. Mexican American. Contemporary Realistic Fiction.105 pp. ISBN 0-440-41010-X. RL=E

Rudy Herrera receives an invitation to a pool party from Tiffany Perez, the richest and most popular girl in his class at school. At first, he doesn't even know what a pool party is. When he finds out, he enlists the help of his friend Alex to acquire the best thing to take to the party, which turns out to be a huge inner tube. Despite some snobbery from some of the other children at the party, Tiffany is genuinely welcoming and friendly toward Rudy. The inner tube is a big attraction as a pool toy for Tiffany and therefore for all the other party goers. This is an interesting story about a boy's crossing the border of economic class for an afternoon by traveling from one neighborhood to another. The story is filled with cultural details that enrich the characterization, plot, and settings. This book is a sequel to Soto's *Boys at Work* (1996, ISBN 0-440-41221-8).

Soto, Gary. (1991). *Taking Sides.* San Diego: Harcourt Brace Jovanovich, Publishers. (PB). Novel. Contemporary Realistic Fiction. Mexican American. 138 pp. ISBN 0-15-284077. RL=M

Lincoln Mendoza is a Mexican American eighth grader and talented basketball player. He lives with his mother, a graphic artist who has started her own graphics business and works very hard. Lincoln and his mother have moved from an urban barrio in The Mission District of San Francisco to Sycamore, a suburban town ten miles south of San Francisco. Lincoln plays basketball for his new school, which brings him into conflict, because his old and new schools play against each other in a league game. Lincoln faces this conflict and learns about loyalty, change, and friendship. His experiences help him to grow stronger. Spanish words and phrases are included in the story, and they are translated in the glossary. In this compelling, richly detailed story, Soto creates a believable picture of the stresses that crossing borders can place on children.

Thomasma, Kenneth. (1993). *Kunu: Escape on the Missouri.* Illustrated by Craig Fleuter. Jackson, WY: Grandview Publishing Company. (PB). Novel. Historical Fiction. Native American. 136 pp. ISBN 0-8010-8892-5. RL=M

Ten-year-old Kunu and his family are part of a group of 2,000 innocent Winnebago Indians who are forcibly removed by the U.S. government from their Minnesota homeland after a Sioux uprising in 1862. They are marched to Crow Creek. The ordeal of removal and resettlement is difficult. Only about 1,350 survive. Kunu and his grandfather Chokay escape in a dugout canoe and make their way home on the Missouri River. On the way, they aid an ailing Euro-American child whose wealthy family shows its gratitude by helping Kunu and Chokay finish their journey on a steamboat and get resettled in their homeland. Eventually, the family is reunited on a new farm.

Whelan, Gloria. (1993). *Night of the Full Moon.* Illustrated by Leslie Bowman. New York: Alfred A. Knopf, Inc. (HB). New York: Random House,

A Stepping Stone Book, 1996. (PB). Novella. Historical Fiction. Native American & Euro-American. 64 pp. ISBN 0-679-88411-4. RL=E

Libby Mitchell, a Euro-American pioneer girl, lives with her family in southern Michigan. She is friends with Fawn, a Potawatomi Indian girl. In the summer of 1840, U.S. soldiers round up and force over five hundred Potawatomis to march to a reservation in Kansas. Because of Libby's friendship with Fawn, she is directly involved in this upheaval and forced migration instigated by the U.S. government. In the end, because Libby's mother had once saved Fawn's life when she was ill, Fawn's father leads his family and Libby to escape the soldiers, and returns Libby to her family. There are details embedded within this story that show the conflict between Euro-American and Native American cultures.

Yep, Laurence. (1991). *The Star Fisher.* New York: William Morrow and Company, Inc. (HB). New York: Penguin Group, Puffin Books, 1992. (PB). Novel. Historical Fiction. Chinese American. 150 pp. ISBN 0-14-036003-4. RL=M

This is the story of the Lee family, a Chinese American family that moves in 1927 from Ohio to Clarksburg, West Virginia in order to open a laundry and start a new life. Joan Lee is in high school and her younger brother and sister are in grammar school. Joan shows intelligence, courage, and humor as she creates a new life for herself in this small West Virginia town where her family is the only Chinese American family. The children are American born and speak English. The parents immigrated from China and do not speak English very well. Yep shows the language difference by the use of italics. Dialogue between the children and English speakers in English or that English speakers carry on among themselves is written in italics. Conversations within the family are not in italics, and although these are written in English, it is to be assumed that the characters are speaking Chinese to one another. This story is based on Yep's own family history.

Crossing Global Borders

Ackerman, Karen. (1994). *The Night Crossing.* Illustrated by Elizabeth Sayles. New York: Scholastic Inc. Novella. Historical Fiction. European Jewish/Holocaust. 56 pp. ISBN 0-590-62430-X. RL=E

It is 1938. Clara's family lives in Austria and her father realizes that they must leave before it is too late, because the Nazis are becoming more powerful daily. Clara has two dolls that she takes with her on her family's perilous journey to freedom in Switzerland. These same two dolls had accompanied Clara's grandmother as a child when she had to flee Russia during one of the pogroms. The dolls turn out to be the perfect hiding place for Mama's special silver candlesticks, and they help Clara have the courage she needs to face the dangers of the journey.

Baillie, Allan. (1985). *Little Brother.* Scotland: Blackie & Son, Ltd. (HB). New York: Puffin Books, 1994. (PB). Novel. Contemporary Realistic Fiction. Cambodian. 144 pp. ISBN 0-14-036862-0. RL=D

Vithy and his older brother Mang escape a brutal Cambodian prison camp, but the soldiers chase them and separate them. Vithy hears a shot and thinks that Mang has been killed. Then, he refuses to believe Mang has died and stubbornly clings to this belief as he makes his way to the Thailand border camp. It is an arduous and dangerous journey, but he makes it. Once in the camp, he is befriended by Dr. Betty, who tries to help him locate Mang. When Vithy has given up hope of ever finding his brother, Dr. Betty arranges for Vithy to accompany her home to Australia. Shortly before their departure, Dr. Betty learns that miraculously Mang has been flown from Bangkok to Sydney for a life-saving operation, but she doesn't tell Vithy. Mang has recuperated enough to be at the airport when Dr. Betty and Vithy arrive, and the book ends with their joyful reunion.

Berry, James. (1992). *Ajeemah and His Son.* New York: HarperCollins, Publishers. (HB). New York: Harper Trophy, 1994. (PB). Novella. Historical Fiction. African/Jamaican. 83 pp. ISBN 0-06-440523-0. RL=M

One day in 1807, while they are on their way to take a dowry of gold to Atu's prospective in-laws, Ajeemah and his eighteen-year-old son Atu are kidnapped by slavers. They are taken from their home in Africa to be sold on the island of Jamaica in the Caribbean. Ajeemah's gold is hidden in his sandals, and he manages to keep that gold by hiding it during all his days as a slave. Atu and Ajeemah are bought by different plantation owners who live only twenty miles apart, but they never see one another again. They both struggle against the enslavement which has been forced upon them. After enduring brutality at the hands of his owners, Atu kills himself. Ajeemah is on the brink of going mad when he is visited by Belle, a slave woman on the same plantation, and they fall in love. Eventually, Ajeemah marries Belle, and they have a daughter. In 1838, freedom comes to the slaves who are living on Caribbean islands under British rule. In 1840, when his daughter marries, Ajeemah gives her a special bride-gift, the gold from Africa he has hidden for so long. This gold will enable his daughter and her new husband to buy their own land at the start of their new life together.

Choi, Sook Nyui. (1991). *Year of Impossible Goodbyes.* Boston, MA: Houghton Mifflin Company. (HB). New York: Dell Publishing, a division of Bantam Doubleday Dell Publishing Group, Inc., 1993. (PB). Novel. Contemporary Realistic Fiction. Korean. 169 pp. ISBN 0-440-82468-0. RL=M

This moving story is set in 1945 in North Korea where ten-year-old Sookan and her family are enduring the cruelties of the occupying Japanese forces. Her father is away in Manchuria serving with the resistance forces and her older brothers have been sent to labor camps. When the war ends and the Communists take over North Korea, Sookan and the rest of her family make a desperate and courageous escape to freedom in American-controlled South Korea. The author of this book actually lived through these times and crossed the borders described in this story. She writes with clarity, power, and authenticity as she creates each character and situation in this story.

The sequel to this book is *Echoes of the White Giraffe* (ISBN 0-440-82525-3). In this book Sookan is now fifteen years old and living with her mother and one of her brothers in Pusan, in South Korea. The Korean War is still raging. The whereabouts of her father and older brothers are still unknown. This is the story of her struggle to survive as a refugee and build a new road for her life.

Conlon-McKenna, Marita. (1991). *Wildflower Girl.* Ireland: O'Brien Press Ltd. (HB). New York: Puffin Books, 1994. (PB). Novel. Historical Fiction. Irish. Immigration to America. 173 pp. ISBN 0-14-036292-4. RL=M

In this sequel to *Under the Hawthorn Tree,* Peggy O'Driscoll is thirteen, orphaned, and lives with her brother Michael, sister Eily, and her great Aunt Nano in the sweet shop in Castletaggart. The landlord serves three weeks notice on Aunt Nano, but in recognition of her forty years of tenancy, offers the family passage to America. In the end, only Peggy, the youngest, goes to America. Eily marries and takes Aunt Nano to live with her. Michael gets a job as a live-in stablehand at a nearby estate. So, with the rest of her family settled, Peggy travels to America alone. The book ends six months after her arrival in Boston where she finds good employment as a live-in housemaid for a wealthy Boston family. Thus, with determination, courage, a willingness to learn and work hard, Peggy triumphs over fear, hardships, and homesickness and succeeds in carving out a new life for herself.

Hansen, Joyce. (1994). *The Captive.* New York: Apple Paperbacks, a trademark of Scholastic Inc. (PB). Novel. Historical Fiction. African American. ISBN 0-590-41624-3. RL=D

This is a compelling story of the slave trade told from the point of view of a twelve-year-old Ashanti boy named Kofi, who is betrayed and sold into slavery in 1788 in West Africa and brought in a slave ship to Boston. The brutal realities of the slave trade are vividly told. The capture, the Middle Passage, and being sold again in the new land are all part of the story. On board the slave ship, Kofi makes two friends, Tim and Joseph, who remain part of his life in the new land. By April, 1789, Kofi and his friends have been purchased by Jonathan and Elizabeth Browne of Salem, Massachusetts. Elizabeth secretly teaches Kofi to read and write, but Jonathan is cruel to the boys. The boys run away, but are intercepted by a ship's captain, Capt. Cuffe, who petitions a court to remand the boys to his custody on the basis of their having been mistreated. The court rules in Capt. Cuffe's favor with respect to Joseph and Kofi. However, because Tim is a European bondservant, he is ordered to stay with Jonathan and Elizabeth Browne. Joseph and Kofi travel to Capt. Cuffe's farm where a new life unfolds for them. In the epilogue, Kofi is grown, married, and a sailor who travels to the shores of Sierra Leone to trade nonhuman cargo. Because he has a new life in Massachusetts, he does not return to his Ashanti village.

Hesse, Karen. (1992). *Letters From Rifka*. New York: Henry Holt and Co. (HB). New York: The Trumpet Club, 1993. (PB). Novel. Historical Fiction. Jewish Immigration to America 148 pp. ISBN 0-440-83050-8. RL=M

This story is written in letter format and is based on the author's family research. The story begins in September of 1919 in Russia and ends in October of 1920 at Ellis Island in New York City. Rifka escapes with her Jewish family from Russia into Poland. She travels with a copy of Pushkin's poems and writes "letters" that chronicle her journey to her cousin Tovah back in Russia. Each chapter is a letter and is headed by a quote from Pushkin's poetry. At one point, while on a train to Warsaw, Rifka befriends a young mother and contracts ringworm from her. This prevents her from traveling with her family to America. Instead, she is sent by the Hebrew Immigrant Aid Society (HIAS) to Belgium, where the HIAS finds her a family to stay with while she receives treatment for her ringworm from the sisters at a nearby convent. When her ringworm is cured, she travels to Ellis Island. She has to overcome some last obstacles, but is finally allowed entry into the United States to join her family. With each physical border she crosses, Rifka grows in courage and self-reliance.

Ho, Minfong. *The Clay Marble*. Canada: HarperCollinsCanadaLtd., 1991. (HB). New York: Farrar Straus Giroux. A Sunburst Book, 1993. (PB).

Novel. Contemporary Realistic Fiction. Cambodian. 163 pp. ISBN 0-374-41229-4. RL=D

In early 1980, twelve-year-old Dara and her family flee their war-torn Cambodian village. They set up a makeshift home in a refugee camp on the Thai-Cambodian border. The camp is shelled and Dara is separated from her family. However, she never gives up searching for them. Through all the death, pain, and struggle she endures because of the war, Dara finds her courage and strength. In the end, she is reunited with her family and instrumental in her family's decision to leave the refugee camp and return to their village to plant, harvest, and begin anew.

Levitin, Sonia. (1970). *Journey to America*. New York: Atheneum Publishers. (HB). New York: Scholastic, Inc., 1987. (PB). Novel. Historical Fiction. Holocaust. Jewish Immigration to America. 150 pp. ISBN 0-590-46728-X. RL=M

In 1938, Lisa Platt and her family are living in Germany. Papa knows that the situation is worsening for Jewish families and so he plans to get his family out of Germany. He makes arrangements for Lisa, her sister Ruth, and Mother to travel to Switzerland and to wait there until he can send for them from America. Then, he leaves for America. Mother, Lisa, and Ruth escape successfully to Switzerland. However, they have to remain there longer than they had planned and their money is depleted. They work together to survive while waiting for word from Papa. Eventually, they are able to make the journey to America and are reunited with Papa.

Lord, Bette Bao. (1984). *In the Year of the Boar and Jackie Robinson*. New York: Harper & Row Publishers. (HB). New York: The Trumpet Club, Bantam Doubleday Dell, 1987. (PB). Novel. Historical Fiction. Chinese American. Immigration to America 169 pp. ISBN 0-440-84182-8. RL=M

This is the story of Shirley Temple Wong's first year of a new life in the United States. Her father, who lives in Brooklyn, sends for Shirley and her mother to join him. The book chronicles Shirley's journey from China, her arrival in the United States, her vain attempts to understand and fit into this new life, and her final success thanks to the miracles of baseball with the Brooklyn Dodgers, Jackie Robinson, and a friendship with an enemy turned ally. Both baseball and her new friend become part of her life as a result of her own perseverance and courage. This book has humor and pathos. The author herself immigrated as a child from China to the United States, and drew on her experiences when writing this work of fiction.

Smucker, Barbara. (1977). *Runaway to Freedom: A Story of the Underground Railway.* United Kingdom: Clarke, Irwin & Company Limited. (HB). New York: Harper Trophy, a division of HarperCollins Publishers, 1979. (PB). Novel. Historical Fiction. African American. 154 pp. ISBN 0-06-440106-5. RL=M

Julilly is tall and strong for her age. She is twelve when she is sold away from her mother in Virginia, and is bought by a plantation owner in Mississippi, where she meets Liza and Lester, fellow slaves. When a Canadian abolitionist, Mr. Ross, in the guise of an ornothologist, visits their plantation, the opportunity arises for Liza, Lester, Julilly, and another slave named Adam to escape. They head north, but the slave catchers find their trail. Hearing the hounds run down Lester and Adam, Liza and Julilly escape detection and press on northward disguised as boys. They are helped along the way by courageous people who are part of the Underground Railway. Finally, they cross the border into Canada and freedom. Julilly is reunited with her mother and Lester, both of whom have also made it to Canada and freedom. Adam is not so lucky apparently, as no mention is made of him. In a note to the reader, the author explains that this fictitious story is based on firsthand experiences found in the narratives of fugitive slaves, on study of the Underground Railroad routes, and on the activities of two historically known abolitionists: Mr. Alexander M. Ross of Canada and Mr. Levi Coffin of Ohio.

Whelan, Gloria. (1992). *Goodbye, Vietnam.* New York: Alfred A. Knopf, Inc. (HB). New York: Random House Books for Young Readers, 1993. (PB). Novel. Contemporary Realistic Fiction. Vietnamese. Immigration to America. 135 pp. ISBN 0-679-823-76X. RL=M

This is the story of Mai and her family and their escape from war-torn Vietnam by boat via Hong Kong to the United States. The book is divided into four sections: The Village, The Journey, The Voyage, and The Silver City. In "The Village," it is shown how the family lived in its own culture. Grandmother is a healer and teller of fortunes and is considered a threat by the new government. To protect Grandmother, the family flees to the sea at Go Cong. In each successive section, the family adjusts to a new "culture" born of the enviornment and situation where they find themselves. As they walk to the sea, they are joined by Bac si Hong, who is a trained medical doctor, and her daughter Kim. Together they board an old boat that is packed with refugees who are all hoping to escape. "The Voyage" tells of the difficult and dangerous voyage to Hong Kong, and the "culture" of life on the boat. In the final part, Mai's family and friends arrive in Hong Kong, or the Silver City. They stay in a huge warehouse with hundreds of other refugees awaiting their fate. Mai remains with her family, but is separated from Bac si Hong and Kim. Later, Bac si Hong is forcefully taken away and is threatened with being returned to Vietnam, because she had tried to help a fellow refugee suffering from appendicitis. Kim rejoins Mai and her family. When Mai and her family receive word that a sponsor has been found for them in America, Kim is included in their travel plans. When the bus is on the way to the airport, Bac si Hong miraculously boards the bus. With the aid of her fellow doctors, she has convinced the authorities not to return her to Vietnam. They all travel to America together.

Yep, Laurence. (1975). *Dragonwings*. New York: Harper & Row, Publishers, Inc. (HB). New York: HarperCollins Children's Books, 1977. (PB). Novel. Historical Fiction. Chinese Immigration. California History. 248 pp. Newbery Honor Book. ISBN 0-06-440085-9. RL=D

Based on an old newspaper article about a young Chinese flyer named Fung Joe Guey, who flew a biplane in the hills of Oakland for twenty minutes on September 22, 1909, this is a story about working to make one's dreams come true. Intrigued by this old newspaper account, Yep uses it as a starting point for this fine piece of historical fiction.

Moon Shadow is eight years old when he sails from China to join his father Windrider, who lives in Chinatown in San Francisco and works in a laundry. Moon Shadow and his father have never met before, but they learn to love and respect each other. Windrider tells Moon Shadow of his belief that he (Windrider) was once a dragon, a belief born of what others call a dream, but which Windrider remembers as a true experience. This story helps Moon Shadow understand his father better. Moon Shadow comes to share Windrider's greatest dream: to build a flying machine. Even though they have to grapple with the challenges of encounters with the Chinese underworld, the earthquake of 1906, poverty, and learning the ways of this new land, Moon Shadow and Windrider work together to realize Windrider's dream. After the San Francisco earthquake of 1906, Windrider and Moon Shadow move to the Oakland hills. Windrider's final flight there is a triumph of the spirit.

Yep, Laurence. (1993). *Dragon's Gate*. New York: HarperCollins Children's Books. (HB). New York: HarperTrophy, 1995. (PB). Novel. Historical Fiction. Chinese Immigration. California History. 275 pp. Newbery Honor Book. ISBN 0-06-440489-7. RL=D

This book is a prequel to *Dragonwings* by Laurence Yep, and is set at the time of the building of the intercontinental railroad linking California to the rest of the United States. Between 1863 and 1865, the Central Pacific, building eastward from California, has laid only thirty-one miles of track. Desperate for laborers to tackle the Sierra Nevada Mountains, the railroad company begins using Chinese crews. At the same time, political unrest in China is causing large numbers of Chinese men to leave China and come to America. Otter is fourteen when he comes to San Francisco looking for the Golden Mountain. He soon joins his father and uncle who are working on the railroad crew in the Sierra Nevada Mountains. Tunneling through the mountain to open the "Dragon's Gate" is difficult, backbreaking, dangerous work. Learning the ways of the new setting in which he finds himself, Otter survives. His father, however, is blinded and his uncle is killed. Instead of returning to China with his father, Otter chooses to stay with the railroad through the winter, hoping to find his uncle's bones in the spring and ship them home to China. Unable to find his uncle's bones, he remains in California instead of returning to China when the work on the railroad is finished.

Chapter 4

Cultural Borders

The titles highlighted in this chapter are nonfiction works of history and biography, works of poetry and/or short stories, and folklore anthologies. These books help expand our understanding of each other across cultural borders. The titles are grouped by the following genres: History, Biography/Autobiography, Poetry and Short Stories, and Folklore Anthologies. The titles are alphabetized by the last name of the author or editor within each genre subcategory.

History

Adler, David A. (1989). *We Remember the Holocaust.* New York: Henry Holt and Company, Inc. (HB). New York: The Trumpet Club, a division of Bantam Doubleday Dell, 1990. (PB). Nonfiction. History. Holocaust/European Jewish. 147 pp. ISBN 0-440-84242-5. RL=D

In his introduction to this compelling and thoroughly researched book, Adler explains that he wrote this book in order to try to answer his own young son's question about what happened in the Holocaust. His research led him to interview both survivors and the children of survivors. Despite the pain of their memories, these people speak because they hope "there will never again be another Holocaust, that once we know where hatred can lead us, we will learn not to hate." (p. xi) The book includes many photographs that visually chronicle the people, places, and events connected to the Holocaust in Europe. The book also includes a chronology of important dates between 1933 and 1945, a glossary, listed further readings, a bibliography of sources, and an index.

Bealer, Alex W. (1972). *Only the Names Remain. The Cherokees and the Trail of Tears.* Boston: Little, Brown and Company. (HB). Boston: Little, Brown and Company, 1996. (PB). Nonfiction. History. Native American. 79 pp. ISBN 0-316-08519-7. RL=E

This is a clearly written history of the Cherokee people before the arrival of Europeans in their world, which changed their way of life forever. The book begins with a chapter about the Cherokee names that remain in use in Georgia where the Cherokees lived for at least a thousand years before the coming of Europeans to the North American continent. It then chronicles the story of the Cherokee struggle to survive as a people as the Euro-Americans took over their lands by any means possible. The famous Cherokee leader Sequoyah, who created a Cherokee alphabet, thus providing his people with a written form of their language, is highlighted as a hero. Then came the forced removal of the Cherokee people from their ancestral lands in Georgia to Arkansas by the U.S. Army under orders instigated by President Andrew Jackson and carried out by his successor, President Martin Van Buren, in 1838. This Trail of Tears, as it is remembered by the Cherokee people, was a killing time for the people. One out of four died on the journey. An index is included in the book.

Brown, Dee. (1974). *Wounded Knee: An Indian History of the American West.* Adapted by Amy Ehrlich. New York: Henry Holt and Company. (HB). New York: Henry Holt, 1994. (PB). Nonfiction. History. Native American. 202 pp. ISBN 0-8050-2700-9. RL=D

This gripping history of Native Americans in conflict with Euro-Americans encroaching upon their lands and lives in the last half of the nineteenth century is divided into two sections. The first section deals with the Navajos and Apaches of the Southwest. The second section deals with the Cheyennes and the Sioux of the Great Plains. The book tells the story of the American West from the Indians' point of view. The point is well made that the events of the twentieth century are connected to the history of the past. The stories of such personalities as General Crook, Tom Jeffords, Cochise, Geronimo, Red Cloud, Sitting Bull, Crazy Horse, and Kicking Bear add to the history presented in this book.

Cox, Clinton. (1991). *Undying Glory: The Story of the Massachusetts 54th Regiment.* New York: Scholastic Inc. (PB). Nonfiction. History. African American. 168 pp. ISBN 0-590-44171-X. RL=M

This is a detailed account of the history of the heroic Massachusetts 54th regiment, which was the first regiment of African Americans to see action as part of the Union Army during the Civil War. The fighting strength of the 54th was severely tested with the assault on Fort Wagner and though they suffered extremely heavy losses, there were some survivors of that bloody, fierce battle. More important, the question of the bravery of black soldiers was put to rest. What the soldiers of the 54th had done with all their heart and effort silenced all doubt. There was no further opposition to allowing black men to fight in the Union Army as soldiers for freedom. The author provides an extensive bibliography and the book is indexed.

Freedman, Russell. (1980). *Immigrant Kids.* New York: Dutton Children's Books. (HB). New York: Scholastic, Inc., 1992. (PB). Nonfiction. History. European Immigration to America. 72 pp. ISBN 0-590-46565-1. RL=E

This book is about the children of the 23 million mostly Southern and Eastern European immigrants who came to the United States between 1880 and 1920. These immigrants shared the common, fervent belief that life in America would be better. Most landed in New York City and passed through Ellis Island. The book covers the journey, the arrival, the living conditions in the immigrant neighborhoods, the school experiences, the work experiences, and the play experiences of the immigrant children. This book is illustrated with photographs taken during the late 1800s and early 1900s depicting the lives of these immigrant children. Sources are cited and the book is indexed.

Johnston, Norma. (1995). *Remember the Ladies: The First Women's Rights Convention.* New York: Scholastic, Inc. (PB). Nonfiction. History. Euro-American. Women's Rights. 170 pp. ISBN 0-590-47086-8. RL=M

This is the story of the first convention organized by women to discuss the rights of women in 1848. Women's rights was an alien concept at the time. This first meeting was held in the summer in the town of Seneca Falls, New York. At that meeting were Lucretia Mott and the African American abolitionist Frederick Douglass. The book focuses on the enthusiastic organizer, Elizabeth Cady Stanton, who continued to actively work for women's rights long after the end of that first convention. The book includes a chronology of important dates, endnotes for quotations, a bibliography, and an index.

Katz, William Loren. (1993). *A History of Multicultural America: Minorities Today.* Austin, TX: Raintree Steck-Vaughn Publishers. (PB). Series: A History of Multicultural America. Nonfiction. History. Multiethnic. ISBN 0-8114-2918-0. RL=M

Part of a series, this book presents a pluralistic overview of the contemporary population in the United States of America. The book focuses on the contributions to American life made by Americans from various cultural backgrounds, including Hispanic Americans, Asian Americans, Russian and Irish immigrants, Native Americans, African Americans, Americans from the West Indies, and women across cultures. It deals with issues of racism and prejudice in contemporary American life. The book is indexed and includes a list for further reading.

Lai, Him Mark, Lim, Genny, and Yung, Judy. (1996). *Island: Poetry and History of Chinese Immigrants on Angel Island, 1910–1940.* (Originally published 1980 by the History of Chinese Detained on Island Project.) Seattle: University of Washington Press. (PB). Nonfiction. History and Poetry. Chinese American. 175 pp. ISBN 0-295-97109-6. RL=D

From 1910 to 1940, Angel Island in San Francisco Bay served as a detainment center for Chinese immigrants. The immigrants were detained for a period of a few days to three years. Thirty years after the detainment center was closed, a park ranger noticed characters written on the walls. He thought they had historical significance and sought help in preserving these writings, which turned out to be poems. More than 135 poems have been recorded; they preserve an astonishing record of courage and spirit in the face of hardship, deprivation, and prejudice. The book includes a history of Chinese immigration, with a particular focus on the years during which Angel Island was in operation. Interviews with survivors of Angel Island and translations of the poems make this a stunning work.

Lester, Julius. (1968). *To Be a Slave.* Illustrated by Tom Feelings. New York: Dial Books for Young Readers. (HB). New York: Scholastic Inc. (PB). Nonfiction. History. African American. 160 pp. Newbery Honor Book. ISBN 0-590-42460-2. RL=D

Julius Lester read through six thousand manuscript pages of slave narratives written down during the 1930s WPA Federal Writers' Project. He then selected from these narratives and organized them for this book, which presents the lived-through experiences of slavery from importation to emancipation told through the stories of ex-slaves and the descendants of slaves. Lester has edited punctuation and spelling for ease of reading. This book provides students with the opportunity to read powerful original resources on the topic of slavery in the United States of America. Lester writes cohesive transition and explanatory material to tie the narratives together. Tom Feelings's illustrations in black and white linger in the mind long after the eye has left the page.

Levine, Ellen. (1993). *Freedom's Children: Young Civil Rights Activists Tell Their Own Stories.* New York: G.P. Putnam's Sons. (HB). New York: Avon Books, 1994. (PB). Nonfiction. History. African American. 162 pp. ISBN 0-380-72114-7. RL=D

This book gives thirty African Americans who were children or teenagers during the 1950s and 1960s the opportunity to tell their compelling stories of what it was like to live in the segregated southern United States and through the tumultous time of the Civil Rights Movement, which resulted in federal legislation to end segregated public facilities such as schools, buses, restaurants, and movie theatres. The author interviewed the storytellers in this book for hours and hours. The book is organized by sections that include stories about experiences of segregation, the beginnings of the Civil Rights Movement, segregation and integration of schools, other forms of protest, and specific events that occurred during that time in American history. The book includes a chronology of events, brief biographical notes on the thirty participant story tellers, a bibliography, and an index.

McKissack, Patricia, and McKissack, Frederick, Jr. (1994). *Black Diamond: The Story of the Negro Baseball Leagues.* New York: Scholastic, Inc. (PB). Nonfiction. History. African American. 184 pp. ISBN 0-590-45810-8. RL=M

This book tells the story of the Negro Baseball Leagues. The combination of the authors' meticulous research and readable text results in a fine piece of informative prose accompanied by documentary photographs. The Negro Baseball Leagues came into existence after the Civil War, when people of color were excluded from playing baseball on teams connected to the National Association of Baseball Players. This exclusion occurred even though prior to the Civil War there had been integrated teams in the North. However, African Americans continued to play the game by forming their own teams and leagues and competing with each other for championships. The Negro Baseball Leagues lasted until the mid-1950s. The decline of the Negro Baseball Leagues began at the end of World War II when Branch Rickey signed Jackie Robinson away from the Kansas City Monarchs (Negro Leagues) to play for the Brooklyn Dodgers. After that, African American players steadily integrated mainstream major league baseball. The authors include a profile of players, a historical timeline, and a bibliography for further reading.

McKissack, Patricia C. and McKissack, Fredrick L. (1996). *Rebels Against Slavery: American Slave Revolts.* New York: Scholastic, Inc. (PB). Nonfiction. History. African American. 182 pp. ISBN 0-590-45736-5. RL=M

This book chronicles the ongoing battle for freedom fought by African slaves in the Americas throughout the seventeenth and eighteenth centuries, finally ending with the period of the Civil War in the United States. There are chapters telling the stories of Toussaint L'Ouverture, Gabriel Prosser, Denmark Vesey, Nat Turner, Cinque, Harriet Tubman, and others. A chronology of important dates marks a revolt of African slaves on Christopher Columbus's son's plantation on Hispaniola in 1522 as the beginning of the rebellion and ends with the passage of the Thirteenth Amendment to the U.S. Constitution in 1865. The book includes a bibliography of related readings and it is indexed.

Myers, Walter Dean. (1991). *Now Is Your Time! The African-American Struggle for Freedom.* New York: HarperCollins. (HB). New York: HarperTrophy, 1991. (PB). Nonfiction. History. African American. 292 pp. Coretta Scott King Award. ISBN 0-06-446120-3. RL=M

In his introduction, Myers states that "what we understand of our history is what we understand of ourselves" (p. ix). This well-researched, highly literate book provides much needed background and perspective concerning the history of the United States. It tells of the African American struggle for freedom throughout American history. Myers uses illustrative examples of the entanglement of the lives of early Africans and European settlers before the American Revolution, as well as African Americans and Euro-Americans after the American Revolution. These examples come from stories gleaned from documents of the time, stories of known historical figures (such as Abd al-Rahman Ibrahima, James Forten, John Brown, Nat Turner, and others), and stories from his own family research. These stories parallel the broader history being depicted and add a rich layer to the book. There is a selected bibliography on related topics and an index.

Stanley, Jerry. (1992). *Children of the Dust Bowl: The True Story of the School at Weedpatch Camp.* New York: The Trumpet Club. (PB). Nonfiction. History. Euro-American. 86 pp. ISBN 0-440-83043-5. RL=E

The first half of this book gives the historical background of the migration of thousands of poor families from the "Dustbowl" of Oklahoma,

Kansas, Nebraska, and parts of Colorado to California during the late 1930s. It tells of the heartbreak, hard times, and humiliation suffered by these people in their quest for a new life in their own country. The second half focuses on the inspiring story of the positive impact one person can have on many lives by telling the story of Leo Hart and his wife Edna, who together made the dream of going to school a reality for the migrant children of Kern County's Weedpatch Camp. Under Mr. Hart's able leadership, a talented and dedicated faculty was assembled. The children, their families, the faculty, and Mr. Hart literally built and ran the school themselves. It existed for four years as an emergency entity until the public school district absorbed it, because so many non-migrant parents were clamoring for their children to be able to attend this special school with its enriched curriculum. Unfortunately, the school wasn't the same after that, but the work Leo Hart had envisioned of providing an environment in which the children could grow, learn, and develop self-worth had already been done. The migrant children of all ages who attended that school during those four years had learned a most important lesson: "They were as good as anybody else" (p. 70). The book ends by citing the accomplishments of many of those children who, as adults, made positive contributions to society in the United States. Leo Hart died at ninety-one years of age on May 30, 1989, and his partner and beloved wife Edna died two months later.

Biography/Autobiography

Drucker, Malka and Halperin, Michael. (1993). *Jacob's Rescue: A Holocaust Story*. New York: Bantam Books for Young Readers. (HB). New York: Dell Publishing, a division of Bantam Doubleday Dell Publishing Group, Inc., 1994. (PB). Nonfiction. Biography. European Jewish/Holocaust. 117 pp. ISBN 0-440-40965-9. RL=E

This inspiring story begins in 1939. Eight-year-old Jacob Gutgeld lives with his well-to-do Jewish family in Warsaw, Poland. When the Nazis invade Poland, his whole life changes. The Nazis take over Jewish homes and businesses and force the Jews to live in ghettos or send them to the death camps. In 1941, Jacob is living with his aunt and grandmother, the only members of his family who are left, in a one-room apartment in the Warsaw ghetto. His mother had died earlier giving birth to his brother David, who had been sent away to the country for safety when his father and uncles had fled Poland the previous year thinking that no one was monstrous enough to make war against women and children. The situation is becoming bleaker by the day in the ghetto. Jacob's aunt arranges for him to be taken in by a Polish Christian couple, Alex and Mela Roslan, who live outside the ghetto and agree to hide and care for him. Eventually, David also joins the Roslan household. Because of the Roslan's willingness to sacrifice and take perilous risks for their own safety, as well as that of their family, Jacob and David survive the Holocaust. Jacob is confronted with many dangerous and frightful times throughout this story, but with courage overcomes his fears and learns to trust and love the Roslan family. The Roslans believe in the common humanity of people and that what the Nazis are doing is wrong. They act on their belief.

Ferris, Jeri. (1991). *Native American Doctor: The Story of Susan Laflesche Picotte*. Minneapolis, MN: Carolrhoda Books, Inc. (HB). Minneapolis, MN: First Avenue Editions, 1991. (PB). Biography. Native American/Omaha. ISBN 0-87614-548-9. RL=E

Ferris, a Euro-American, provides a bibliography listing books, articles, manuscripts, and interviews she conducted in order to bring sensitivity and authenticity to her writing of this inspirational, heroic Native American woman's life. Dr. Picotte lived from 1865 until 1915, and saw the end of her Omaha people's traditional way of life. Her parents encouraged her to become educated in the ways of the white man's world. She overcame many obstacles to attend and graduate from Women's Medical College of Pennsylvania. She then dedicated her life to being of service to her people as a doctor. The book is indexed.

Filipovic, Zlata. (1994). *Zlata's Diary*. New York: Viking Penguin. (HB). New York: Scholastic, Inc., 1994. (PB). Nonfiction. Autobiography. European Bosnian. 200 pp. ISBN 0-590-48792-2. RL=M

Zlata is a thirteen-year-old Bosnian girl living in Sarajevo with her parents. Zlata's family is relatively well off. She begins keeping a diary in September of 1991, a few months before the barricades go up in Sarajevo and the heavy shelling begins. Calling her diary Mimmy, she writes of ordinary concerns in her thirteen-year-old life such as pop music, movies, boys and girls she knew, skiing, and holidays. However, within six months of her first entry, she writes of the horrors and deprivations that have become her life. She and her family struggle to survive and to maintain hope and some shred of normalcy amid the madness of war. Janine di Giovanni, a journalist, is instrumental in helping Zlata and her parents escape Sarajevo under French protection. Zlata agrees to have her diary published as a book for all the children still trapped in the hell of Sarajevo, as well as for those who have already died in the war.

Freedman, Russell. (1987). *Indian Chiefs.* New York: Holiday House. (HB). New York: Scholastic, Inc., 1991. (PB). Nonfiction. Biography. Native American. 151 pp. ISBN 0-590-45357-2. RL=M

This book tells of the end of the traditional way of life of Native Americans through the stories of six extraordinary men, chiefs among their people. The six chiefs are Red Cloud of the Oglala Sioux, Satanta of the Kiowas, Quanah Parker of the Comanches, Washakie of the Shoshones, Joseph of the Nez Perce, and Sitting Bull of the Hunkpapa Sioux. The book includes many stunning photographs of Native Americans and others who lived during their times. There is a bibliography of research resources and photographic resources, as well as an index.

Freedman, Russell. (1996). *The Life and Death of Crazy Horse.* Illustrations by Amos Bad Heart Bull. New York: Holiday House. (HB). New York: Scholastic Inc., 1997. (PB). Nonfiction. Biography. Native American. Oglala Sioux. ISBN 0-590-39731-1. RL=M

This is a well-researched, articulate, respectful biography about Crazy Horse, who was a leader of the Oglala Sioux throughout the 1860s until his death in 1877. Freedman explains in detail the sources of his material for this biography. He credits the work from the 1930s of Eleanor Hinman and Mari Sandoz, who traveled throughout Sioux country interviewing surviving friends and relatives of Crazy Horse, as having been most helpful in writing this biography. As far as is known, Crazy Horse never allowed himself to be photographed, so it is fitting that there are no photos in the book. The drawings by Amos Bad Heart Bull add depth to the text. A chronology, a selective bibliography, and an index are included.

Hautzig, Esther. (1968). *The Endless Steppe: Growing Up in Siberia.* New York: HarperCollins Children's Books. (HB). New York: HarperTrophy, a division of HarperCollins Publishers, n.d. (PB). Nonfiction. Autobiography. European Jewish. ISBN 0-06-440577-X. RL=D

In 1941, the Russians invade Vilna, Poland, where the wealthy Jewish Rudomin family lives. The family is declared to be made up of capitalists and, as such, to be enemies of the people. They are loaded onto cattle cars and shipped to Siberia, where they struggle to exist for the remainder of World War II. As difficult as their exile is, being in Siberia keeps them from being sent to one of Hitler's concentration camps, like so many of their fellow countrymen. The story of this family's ordeal is told from ten-year-old Esther's point of view.

Hilts, Len. (1987). *Quanah Parker.* San Diego, CA: An Odyssey/Great Episodes Book, Harcourt Brace Jovanovich, Publishers. (PB). Biography. Native American. Comanche. ISBN 0-15-264447. RL=M

Quanah Parker was the son of the Comanche Chief Peta Nocona and a Euro-American woman captured as a child and adopted by the Comanches named Cynthia Ann Parker. Her Comanche name was Naudah. Quanah became a warrior chief of the Comanches. He belonged to the Quohadas, the last band of the Comanches to come in off the plains and cease fighting. It was Quanah who led the Comanches in war against the Euro-Americans, as well as later in the struggle to establish a new life after surrender. Quanah became a judge and a successful, respected rancher who lived in a large Euro-American-style ranch house called Star House, where he once entertained President Teddy Roosevelt. The later years of Quanah's life were spent helping his people bridge the gap between their vanished traditional way of life and the new life of ranching on the reservation. He was the last chief of the Comanches.

Houston, Jeanne Wakatsuki and Houston, James D. (1973). *Farewell to Manzanar.* San Francisco Book Co./Houghton Mifflin edition. (HB). New York: Bantam Starfire Book, 1974. (PB). Nonfiction. Autobiography. Japanese American. 145 pp. ISBN 0-553-27258-6. RL=D

This is a revealing, heart-rending story of a young Japanese American girl and her family as they cope with internment and re-entry into a free life in the United States during and immediately after World War II. The dignity and courage with which they face the ordeal of internment and the difficulties of re-entering a free life after the camp are inspirational. This book deals with issues of prejudice and racism that are still pertinent now.

Kroeber, Theodora. (1964). *Ishi, Last of His Tribe.* Boston: Houghton Mifflin Company. (HB). New York: Bantam Books, a division of Bantam Doubleday Dell Publishing Group, Inc., 1989. (PB). Nonfiction. Biography. Native American/Yahi of California. 213 pp. ISBN 0-553-24898-7. RL=D

This is the story of Ishi, who was born in 1861 or 1862, and lived with his family in the ancient ways of the Yahi in the western foothills of Mount Lassen in northern California. By the time Ishi was ten years old, most of his people had been killed or driven from their lands by the Saldu (white men), whose greed for gold had brought them into the hills of the Yana. Ishi and his small family struggled to survive and to honor the ancient ways, while remaining hidden from the eyes of the Saldu. However, by the early 1900s, Ishi was living alone, the last one of his people. He struggled on until he was nearly dead from grief and starvation. At that point, he stumbled into the Saldu world. In 1911, Ishi was found in the corral of a slaughterhouse in Oroville. He eventually wound up living at the newly established Museum of Anthropology at the University of California in Berkeley, California, under the protection of Theodora Kroeber's husband, Alfred Kroeber, curator of the museum. Ishi lived long enough to tell his story and leave us a record of how his people had lived. He died at the museum in March, 1916. A glossary of Yahi words is included.

McKissack, Patricia and McKissack, Fredrick. (1992). *Sojourner Truth: Ain't I a Woman?* New York: Scholastic, Inc. (PB). Nonfiction. Biography. African American. 186 pp. ISBN 0-590-44691-6. RL=M

This well-written biography was thoroughly researched. In 1797, Isabella, called Belle, was born a slave in New York. After she was freed in 1827, she renamed herself Sojourner Truth, and started a new life. She became a preacher, an abolitionist, an activist for the rights of both blacks and women. She was a powerful speaker with a profound faith in God, and she stirred audiences everywhere she spoke. She lived until 1883, thus seeing the end of slavery in the United States. The book is indexed and includes biographical information about key historical figures who lived during Sojourner Truth's lifetime, such as Susan B. Anthony and Frederick Douglass.

Palacios, Argentina. (1994). *Standing Tall: The Stories of Ten Hispanic Americans.* New York: Scholastic, Inc. (PB). Nonfiction. Biography. Scholastic Biography Series. Hispanic American. 234 pp. ISBN 0-590-47140-6. RL=M

This is a collection of short biographies of the following Hispanic Americans: David G. Farragut, Severo Ochoa, Jaime Escalante, Roberto Clemente, Vilma S. Martinez, Antonia C. Novello, Franklin R. Chang-Diaz, Fernando Bujones, Miriam Santos, and Gloria Estefan. A selected bibliography and sources connected to each individual is included. The book is indexed.

Parks, Rosa with Haskins, Jim. (1992). *Rosa Parks: My Story.* New York: Dial Books for Young Readers. (HB). New York: Scholastic Inc., 1994. (PB). Nonfiction. Autobiography. African American. 192 pp. ISBN 0-590-46538-4. RL=M

With power and eloquence, Rosa Parks tells her own story about her childhood, education, marriage, and work as an activist prior to that fateful day on the bus in Montgomery, including her work as the secretary of the NAACP in Montgomery, Alabama. She recounts the fateful incident at the end of her work day on December 1, 1955, when she refused to give up her seat to a white man. She explains that she was not any more physically tired than she usually was at the end of a work day, but that she was very tired of "giving in" (p. 116). She made a conscious choice, and although she said she couldn't see ahead to all the consequences of that choice, it was a choice grounded in her background and experiences that led up to that moment.

Pelz, Ruth. (1990). *Black Heroes of the Wild West.* Illustrated by Leandro Della Piana. Seattle, WA: Open Hand Publishing, Inc. (PB). Nonfiction. Biography. African American. 57 pp. ISBN 0-940880-26-1. RL=E

This collection of short biographies about nine African Americans who played a role in the history of the American West includes the following: Estevan (c.1501–1539), Jean Baptiste Point Du Sable (1745–1818), George Washington Bush (c. 1779–1863), James Beckwourth (1798–1866), Clara Brown (1803–1885), Biddy Mason (1820–1891), Mifflin Gibbs (1823–1903), Mary Fields (b.?–1914), and Bill Pickett (c.1870–1932). These brief biographies could be used to introduce students to these men and women who made contributions of various kinds to the history of the American West. The author includes a bibliography of juvenile literature (categorized as appropriate for high school and below) and adult literature connected to people in this book.

Pettit, Jayne. (1993). *A Place to Hide: True Stories of Holocaust Rescues.* New York: Scholastic, Inc. (PB). Nonfiction. Biography. Scholastic Biography Series. European Jewish/Holocaust. 114 pp. ISBN 0-590-45353-X. RL=M

Included within this book are the rescue stories of (1) Miep Santrouschitz of Amsterdam, who hid the Frank family when the Nazis invaded Holland, (2) Oskar and Emilie Schindler, (3) the work of the Christian Danes to save the Jewish Danes by smuggling them across the sea to Sweden, (4) the efforts of the people of the village of Le Chambon in the mountains of Southern France, (5) Padre Niccacci's underground operation in Assisi, Italy, and (6) the dedication of Madame Marie to save Jewish children in Paris. A bibliography of sources and an index are included.

Uchida, Yoshiko. (1987). *The Invisible Thread.* New York: Simon & Schuster Books for Young Readers. (HB). Needham, MA: Silver Burdett Ginn, n.d. (PB). MultiSource Literature Set, Silver Burdett Ginn. Nonfiction. Autobiography. Japanese American. 136 pp. ISBN 0-663-58565-1. RL=D

In this stunning autobiography, the author writes with powerful clarity about her life. She recounts her experiences growing up as a Japanese American girl in Berkeley, California in the 1930s. She writes of her family and their lives together in such a way that one feels as if one has been a guest in the Uchida home. She tells about how, during the years of World War II, she and her family suffered the deprivation and humiliation of internment. She ends this book by telling of the end of internment for her family and the beginning of their new life together. *A Jar of Dreams* (ISBN 0-689-71672-9), *The Best Bad Thing* (ISBN 0-689-71745-8), and *Journey Home* (ISBN 0-395-45995-8) are works of fiction of Ms. Uchida's appropriate for inclusion in the fourth- through sixth-grade curriculum. There is a complete list of Ms. Uchida's many fine works for children at the end of this autobiography.

Watkins, Yoko Kawashima. (1986). *So Far From the Bamboo Grove*. New York: Lothrop, Lee & Shepard Books. (HB). New York: A Beech Tree Paperback Book, 1994. (PB). Nonfiction. Autobiography. Japanese. World War II. 183 pp. ISBN 0-688-13115-8. RL=D

This is a story of courage and survival amidst war, the greatest clash of cultures. In July of 1945, Yoko (Japanese) is eleven years old and living with her mother and sixteen-year-old sister Ko in Northern Korea, within fifty miles of the Manchurian border. Her father is a Japanese government official working in Manchuria, but he does not agree with the decisions that have plunged Japan into war with Russia and the United States. Yoko's eighteen-year-old brother Hideyo volunteers for the Japanese army during the last days of the war. As the Americans bomb Japan, the Korean Communists move to establish themselves in North Korea and they hate the Japanese, so Yoko, her mother, and sister have to flee for their lives and hope that one day they will be reunited with their loved ones. They finally reach Japan. As they struggle to survive in war-torn Japan, Mother dies. The two girls are left on their own. Eventually, their brother Hideyo also returns to Japan. In a postscript note, we learn that Yoko's father returns to Japan from a Siberian prison camp six years after the events recounted in this book. There is a publisher's note at the end that provides more of the historical background of the Korean/Japanese relationship.

Yates, Elizabeth. (1950). *Amos Fortune Free Man*. Illustrated by Nora S. Unwin. New York: E.P. Dutton. (HB). New York: Puffin Books, a division of Penguin Books USA, Inc., 1989. (PB). Biography. African American. 181 pp. Newbery Award. ISBN 0-14-034158-7. RL=D

The original Amos Fortune papers form the basis of the primary source material for this book. These papers are quoted within the context of the story. If an African American author were to write this book today, there would probably be differences in the way Amos Fortune's story would be told from an insider's perspective. However, the book is included in this collection because the author wrote with respect for and knowledge of Amos Fortune based on her research. Also, the book was extremely unusual in the field of children's literature at the time of its original publication in 1950.

Amos Fortune was a free African who was captured as a teenager and sold into slavery about 1725. He survived the horrors of the Middle Passage and arrived in Boston, where he was purchased by a Quaker man named Copeland. He was the Copeland family slave for about fifteen years until Mr. Copeland died. All those years, he worked with Mr. Copeland and learned the weaving trade, as well as how to read and write, from Mrs. Copeland. In 1740, upon Mr. Copeland's death, Mrs. Copeland sold him to Mr. Richardson, a tanner from nearby Woburn. In 1763, Mr. Richardson set up the means by which Amos could buy his own freedom using money he earned here and there with his skills as a tanner learned from Mr. Richardson. This document survived Mr. Richardson. When he died, Mrs. Richardson quitclaimed any further payments, and drew up her own manumission paper for Amos, granting him his freedom in May, 1769.

The second half of the story tells about what Amos did with his freedom, going on to live a life of hard work, service to others, and devotion to his family. This is an inspiring story of a man of great dignity, intelligence, perseverance, and humanity.

Yep, Laurence. (1991). *The Lost Garden*. New York: Julian Messner, a division of Simon & Schuster. (HB). New York: A Beech Tree Paperback Book, 1996. (PB). Nonfiction. Autobiography. Chinese American. 124 pps. ISBN 0-688-13701-6. RL=D

Using his masterful gifts as a storyteller, Yep is boldly honest about his frequently painful journey to learn acceptance of self and how he fits into the patchwork quilt of American society. He describes himself as a Chinese American child who grew up in a black neighborhood, as being too American for Chinatown and too Chinese for everywhere else (first page, unnumbered). He also connects the stories from his own family to the history of Chinese immigration into the United States. As he sorts through his experiences and his family's experiences in America (the

United States), he shows us what it means to him to be a Chinese American. Woven throughout his story are his thoughts related to the power of writing and the power of memory as seed energy for the writer. This would be an excellent book to include in an author study of Yep.

Poetry and Short Stories

Adoff, Arnold. (1982). *All the Colors of the Race.* Illustrated by John Steptoe. New York: Lothrop, Lee & Shepard Books. (HB). New York: Beech Tree Edition, 1992. (PB). Poetry. African American and Jewish. Universal. 56 pp. ISBN 0-688-11496-2. RL=M

In this thought-provoking collection of thirty-seven poems dedicated to his own two biracial children, Adoff invites the reader to see into the hearts and souls of others, particularly biracial children. He celebrates the spectrum of the human race by including diverse life experiences and histories from his own family. The poems in this uplifting collection are focused on love and the power that comes from acknowledging and celebrating differences, while at the same time celebrating the universality of being a member of the human race. It is a positive, poetic depiction of crossing ethnic borders within a family.

Altman, Susan and Lechner, Susan. (1993). *Followers of the North Star. Rhymes About African American Heroes, Heroines, and Historical Times.* Illustrated by Byron Wooden. Chicago: Children's Press. (PB). Poetry. African American. 48 pp. Series: *Many Voices, One Song.* ISBN 0-516-45151-0. RL=M

This collection includes poems inspired by well-known African Americans from U.S. history such as George Washington Carver, Benjamin Banneker, Harriet Tubman, Thurgood Marshall, Rosa Parks, Martin Luther King, Jr., Malcolm X, and others. It also includes poems inspired by African Americans prominent in sports and entertainment such as Leontyne Price, Arthur Mitchell, Muhammad Ali, Jackie Robinson, and others. Some poems focus on key contributions of African Americans to U.S. history. These include: "Followers of the North Star," "Buffalo Soldiers," "The Little Rock Nine," and "Sit-Ins." The cultural and historical information in these poems highlights the contributions of African Americans to U. S. history and culture.

Baylor, Byrd. (1997). *The Way to Make Perfect Mountains: Native American Legends of Sacred Mountains.* Illustrations by Leonard F. Chana. El Paso, TX: Cinco Puntos Press. (PB). (Originally published in 1981 by Charles Scribner's Sons as *A God on Every Mountain Top: Stories of Southwest Indian Sacred Mountains.*) Poetry/Legends. Native American. 62 pp. ISBN 0-938317-26-1. RL=E

This moving collection of narrative poems is based on the sacred connections Native Americans feel toward certain mountains. The poems tell the stories of the mountains and the Native Americans who respect them. The poems are grouped thematically. The themes are: Beginnings; Changes; Power, Magic, Mystery and Dreams; and The Beings in the Mountains. The stippled, black and white drawings of Leonard F. Chana add to the quiet power of the collection.

Baylor, Byrd. (1977). *The Way to Start a Day.* Illustrated by Peter Parnall. New York: Atheneum Books for Young Readers. (HB). New York: Aladdin Paperbacks, an imprint of Simon & Schuster, 1986. (PB). Poetry. Global. 32 pp. ISBN 0-689-71054-2. RL=E

Baylor weaves traditions for greeting the day from many cultures past and present into this eloquent narrative poem. Parnall's illustrations add to the energy of the poetry.

Bruchac, Joseph and London, Jonathan. (1992). *Thirteen Moons on Turtle's Back: A Native American Year of Moons.* Illustrated by Thomas Locker. New York: Philomel Books, a division of The Putnam and Grosset Group. (HB). New York: The Trumpet Club, Inc., a division of Bantam Doubleday Dell Publishing Group, Inc., 1995. (PB). Poetry. Native American. 29 pp. ISBN 0-440-83438-4. RL=M

In this beautiful collection of narrative poetry, one moon story is chosen from thirteen different Native American tribal nations from different geographic regions "to give a wider sense of the many things Native American people have been taught to notice in this beautiful world around us" (last page, not numbered). The poems are greatly enhanced by Thomas Locker's paintings.

Carlson, Lori M. and Ventura, Cynthia L., (Eds.). (1990). *Where Angels Glide at Dawn: New Stories From Latin America.* Introduction by Isabel Allende and Illustrations by Jose Ortega. New York: Harper Trophy, a Division of HarperCollins Publishers. (PB). Short Stories. Latin American (various countries of origin). 113 pp. ISBN 0-06-440464-1. RL=M

This superb collection of ten short stories was originally written in Spanish and translated into English for this publication. These powerful stories illuminate the magic that resides beneath the surface of ordinary lives. These stories are grounded in the Latin American cultural belief that magic and ordinary reality are two sides of the same coin of life experience. For instance, in the story "Fairy Tale" by Barbara Mujica, Monica, who lives with her parents, grandmother, and siblings in New York, travels to spend the summer with her relatives in Puerto Rico, the land of her ancestors. While there, she has an experience that blurs the border between physical reality and magical reality, because she encounters a character from one of her grandmother's stories.

Cumpian, Carlos. (1994). *Latino Rainbow.* Illustrated by Richard Leonard. Chicago: Children's Press. (PB). Poetry. Latino/Latina. Series: *Many Voices, One Song.* 48 pp. ISBN 0-516-45153-7. RL=M

This collection includes poems inspired by well-known Hispanic Americans such as Luis Alvarez, Nobel Prize winner; Cesar Chavez, farm worker organizer; Joan Baez, folk singer and civil rights activist; Henry Cisneros, political leader; Antonia Coelho Novello, U.S. Surgeon General; and Ellen Ochoa, first Latina astronaut. There are also poems based on Latino/a connections to American history/culture such as *The California Rancheros, The Treaty of Guadalupe Hidalgo,* and *The Neorican Poets/ Nuyorican Poets.* Information related to the contributions of Hispanic Americans to U.S. history and culture is highlighted by these poems. A glossary is included, because many of the poems contain Spanish words and/or phrases.

George, Chief Dan. (1974). *My Heart Soars.* Illustrated by Helmut Hirnschall. Surry, B.C.: Hancock House Publishers Ltd. (HB). Blaine, WA: Hancock House Publishers, 1994. (PB). 96 pp. Poetry. Native American. ISBN 0-88839-231-1. RL=M

This moving collection of poems and essays reflects the thoughts of this sage Native American poet as he considers his life experience, his people and their history and their connection to nature and all that is. In one of his poems, he urges young Native Americans to write and publish their own poems and stories.

Greenfield, Eloise. (1978). *Honey, I Love and Other Love Poems.* Illustrated by Diane and Leo Dillon. New York: HarperCollins Children's Books, a division of HarperCollins Publishers. (HB). New York: Harper Trophy, 1986. (PB). Poetry. African American. 41 pp. ISBN 0-06-443097-9. RL=E

This collection contains rhythmical, image specific, emotion packed, language-rich poems firmly grounded in the human experiences of love, family, and childhood. The content of some of these poems reflects a specific African American perspective, while other poems reflect a universal perspective using rhythms and images appealing to all children. For instance, *Things* is a powerful poem with universal appeal about the joy of writing poetry. In *Harriet Tubman,* Greenfield focuses her lens on African American history and highlights Harriet Tubman as the heroine of the poem. The poems in this collection beg to be read aloud over and over again.

Greenfield, Eloise. (1988). *Nathaniel Talking.* Illustrated by Jan Spivey Gilchrist. New York: Black Butterfly Children's Books. (PB). Poetry. African American. 32 pp. ISBN 0-86316-201-0. RL=E

Through the poem *Nathaniel's Rap,* Greenfield shows that all these poems are the thoughts, talk, and philosophy of nine-year-old Nathaniel B. Free, the title character. The poems are written in rhythmical, nonrhyming, narrative free verse. They are rich in sensory language and specific images. Many of these poems have a universal appeal because they focus on family, hopes, love, and friendship. Other pieces expand the reader's picture of the specific family and experiences of the character Nathaniel B. Free.

Hirschfelder, Arlene and Singer, Beverly R. (1992). *Rising Voices: Writings of Young Native Americans.* New York: Ivy Books, a division of Ballantine Books. (PB). Essays and Poetry. Native American. 131 pp. ISBN 0-663-58515-5. RL=M 98.

This rich, many-layered collection of poetry, essays, and personal stories was written by young Native Americans. These young writers articulate their feelings on the subjects of identity, family, homelands, ritual and ceremony, education, and harsh realities. This collection invites the reader to cross the border separating the Indian life experience from the non-Indian life experience. In crossing that border, life experiences reaching beyond the borders of any one group of people are waiting to be found. For instance, the Navajo students at the Tohatchi School in New Mexico wrote "If I Were a Pony." Certainly many children from many different life experiences can relate to being wildly free and never thinking of school, as described in this poem.

Hughes, Langston. (1994). *The Dream Keeper and Other Poems.* Illustrated by Brian Pinkney. New York: Alfred A. Knopf, Inc. (HB). New York: A Borzoi Book by Alfred A. Knopf, Inc., 1996. (PB). Poetry. African American. 95 pp. ISBN 0-679-88347-9. RL=E

The poems in this collection were originally published by Alfred A. Knopf in 1932. This recently issued edition, illustrated with the black and white scratchboard art of Brian Pinkney, makes an outstanding contribution to any classroom library or child's bookshelf. This edition includes an Introduction by Lee Bennett Hopkins and A Personal Note by Augusta Baker. This volume contains such classic poems as "The Dream Keeper," "Dreams," "Poem," "The Negro Speaks of Rivers," and "Mother to Son." The stunning new appearance of this classic work enhances these poems which speak to us all.

. . . *I Never Saw Another Butterfly: Children's Drawings and Poems From Terezin Concentration Camp 1942–1944.* (1978). New York: Schocken Books. (PB). Poetry. European Jewish/Holocaust. 80 pp. ISBN 0-8052-0598-5. RL=M

This anthology of drawings and poems presents the voices of children from the Holocaust who spent their final days in Terezin in Czechoslovakia. Of the 15,000 children who lived at Terezin before being transported to death camps, only 100 walked away from Terezin to safety. Most of these children died in 1944, the next to the last year of World War II. Their original drawings and poems have been preserved in the State Jewish Museum in Prague. Their words and images remain a poignant reminder of the strength of the human spirit.

Izuki, Steven. (1994). *Believers in America: Poems About Americans of Asian and Pacific Islander Descent.* Illustrated by Bill Fukuda McCoy. Chicago: Children's Press. (PB). Poetry. Asian and Pacific Islander American. Series: *Many Voices, One Song.* 48 pp. ISBN 0-516-45152-9. RL=M

This collection includes poems inspired by the lives of Asian Americans and Pacific Islander Americans such as Daniel Inouye, Dr. An Wang, Patsy Takemoto Mink, Bruce Lee, Vicki Manalo, Ellison Onizuka, and Kristi Yamaguchi. It also includes poems that focus on events in U.S. history connected to the life experiences of Asian Americans and Pacific Islander Americans from the sixteenth century through the twentieth century. These poems include such titles as "The First Filipinos in North America," "Chinese Railroad Workers," "Angel Island: The Door to America," "Internment of Japanese Americans," "The 100/442nd Regiment," and "Welcome to Chinatown." A glossary of terms is included. These powerful poems highlight the experiences and contributions of Asian Americans and Pacific Islander Americans to the culture and history of the United States.

Johnson, James Weldon. (1921, 1993). *Lift Every Voice and Sing.* Illustrated by Elizabeth Catlett. Introduction by Jim Haskins. New York: Walker & Co., Inc. (HB). New York: Walker & Co., Inc., 1994. (PB). Poetry/Song. African American. 38 pp. ISBN 0-8027-7442-3. RL=D

In his introduction to this classic poem/song, Jim Haskins writes of the history behind the words and music that were written by two brothers, James Weldon Johnson and J. Rosamond Johnson, in 1900, as well as the history of the linocut illustrations created by Elizabeth Catlett in 1946 and 1947. It is noted that although the text and illustrations were created independently, they complement each other perfectly. For decades this poem/song was thought of as the Negro National Anthem. Today, its words about the struggle to overcome oppression with faith and courage and perseverance remain perennially inspiring and reach across cultural borders.

Joseph, Lynn. (1990). *Coconut Kind of Day: Island Poems.* Illustrated by Sandra Speidel. New York: Lothrop, Lee & Shepard Books, a division of William Morrow & Company, Inc. (HB). New York: Puffin Books, a division of Penguin Books USA Inc., 1992. (PB). Poetry. Caribbean Islands. 32 pp. ISBN 0-14-054527-1. RL=M

This rhythmical collection of thirteen delightful poems begins with *Morning Songs* and ends with *Night Songs.* The author captures the colors, rhythms, sounds, sights, and smells of a day in the life of a happy child on a Caribbean island. In an accompanying author's note, the author tells of growing up on the island of Trinidad and vividly remembering those days. She says she wrote the poems so that she would always remember her island and she claims that the scenes in the poems are all true. She explains a few terms that she feels needed explaining because they are specific to her island.

Medearis, Angela Shelf. (1991). *Dancing With the Indians.* Illustrated by Samuel Byrd. New York: Holiday House. (PB). Poetry. African American. Seminole Indian. 32 pp. ISBN 0-8234-1023-4. RL=E

This narrative poem is based on the life of the author's great-grandfather, John Davis, who escaped from slavery around 1862 and traveled to Oklahoma where he married a Seminole Indian woman and had a son. The marriage didn't last and John Davis remarried an African American woman. However, he maintained ties with the Seminole community, traveling twice a year with his wife and their children to join the Indian powwows. This tradition continued into the next generation. The author credits this family history as the inspiration for this narrative poem, which tells of an African American family going to visit their Seminole Indian friends and joining in the Ribbon Dance and the Stomp Dance at a powwow. Samuel Byrd's vivid illustrations enhance the emotional impact of the text.

Myers, Walter Dean. (1995). *Glorious Angels: A Celebration of Children.* New York: HarperCollins Publishers. (PB). Poetry. Global. ISBN 0-06-446726-0. RL=E

In this marvelous collection, Myers uses antique photographs of children from around the world as inspiration for the poems he writes to celebrate all children. The photographs and poems combined together focus on the universality of the wishes, hopes, and dreams of childhood across borders of ethnicity.

Nye, Naomi Shihab. (Ed.). (1992). *This Same Sky: A Collection of Poems From Around the World.* New York: Four Winds Press. 212 pp. (HB). New York: Simon & Schuster Books for Young Readers. (PB). Poetry. Global. ISBN 0-689-80630-2. RL=D

Eastern and Western poets are represented in this book. However, poets born in the United States are excluded from this volume, because the editor feels their work is generally available in other anthologies published in recent years. When it was necessary to translate the poems, the translators' names are included. The poems are grouped thematically using the following themes: Words and Silences, Dreams and Dreamers, Families, This Earth and Sky in Which We Live, Losses, and Human Mysteries. There are many non-rhyming, image-rich poems in this volume, which would make it particularly useful in the classroom as a teaching resource. The many voices found herein reflect the similarities and differences among a variety of human experiences across cultures, thus helping readers cross borders through the vehicle of poetry.

Sneve, Virginia Driving Hawk. (Ed.). (1989). *Dancing Teepees: Poems of American Indian Youth.* Illustrations by Stephen Gammell. New York: Holiday House. (HB). New York: Holiday House, 1989. (PB). Poetry. Native American. 32 pp. ISBN 0-8234-0879-5. RL=E

Some of the poems in this collection were written by specific Native American authors. Other poems are cited as having originated from a particular tribal group and were part of the oral language tradition of that group. All of the poems are rhythmical and image rich and show the beauty and strength of Native American poetry, which remains connected to the oral tradition of stories, songs, and prayers so embedded in Native American cultures.

Soto, Gary. (1990). *Baseball in April and Other Stories.* San Diego, California: Harcourt Brace Jovanovich, Publishers. (HB). San Diego: An Odyssey Book a division of Harcourt Brace Jovanovich, 1991. (PB). Short Stories. Mexican American. 137 pp. ISBN 0-15-205721-8. RL=M

This is a collection of eleven masterful short stories. Using his own experiences growing up in Fresno, California as inspiration, the author depicts the ordinary lives of young people living in that same town. These stories highlight universal themes of youth and age, love and friendship, success and failure, and understanding of oneself and others. The stories realistically illuminate life in a proud, working-class Mexican American family. Soto occasionally uses Spanish in the stories, especially in the dialogue. Usually the meaning can be determined from the context, but a glossary of Spanish words and phrases used in the book is provided at the end.

Soto, Gary. (1992). *Neighborhood Odes.* Illustrated by David Diaz. San Diego, CA: Harcourt Brace Jovanovich, Inc. (HB) New York: Scholastic, Inc., 1994. (PB) Poetry. Mexican American. 68 pp. ISBN 0-590-47335-2. RL=M

In this collection of twenty-one odes, Soto celebrates the commonplace things and events he remembers from his childhood. Spanish words and phrases are used naturally in the titles and texts of the poems, and a glossary is included to aid non-Spanish speaking readers. The poems are rich in sensory language and metaphor. They create specific images connected to lived-through experiences of a childhood that crossed cultural borders.

Strickland, Dorothy S. (Ed.). (1982). *Listen Children: An Anthology of Black Literature.* New York: Bantam Books, Inc. (HB). New York: A Bantam Starfire Book, 1986. (PB). Short Stories/Poetry/Plays. African American. 132 pp. ISBN 0-553-27092-3. RL=M

This is an excellent collection of literature by African Americans focused on values and feelings. It includes poetry by Eloise Greenfield, Langston Hughes, Margaret Walker, and Lucille Clifton, as well as a story by Virginia Hamilton and autobiographical pieces by Maya Angelou and Wilma Rudolph. Dr. Martin Luther King, Jr.'s "I Have a Dream" speech is also in this collection. There is a fine play based on the life of Harriet Tubman called "When the Rattlesnake Sounds" by Alice Childress.

Strickland, Dorothy S. and Strickland, Michael R. (Eds.). (1994). *Families: Poems Celebrating the African American Experience.* Illustrated by

John Ward. Honesdale, Pennsylvania: Wordsong Boyds Mill Press, Inc. (HB). First Wordsong paperback, 1996. (PB). Poetry. African American. 32 pp. ISBN 1-56397-560-2. RL=E

This fine anthology of poetry celebrating families includes poems by Gwendolyn Brooks, Nikki Giovanni, Langston Hughes, Lucille Clifton, and Eloise Greenfield. The editors co-wrote an all-inclusive introductory poem titled "Families, Families."

Thomas, Joyce Carol. (1993). *Brown Honey in Broomwheat Tea*. Illustrated by Floyd Cooper. New York: HarperCollins Publishers. (PB). Poetry. African American. Coretta Scott King Author Award Honor Book and Coretta Scott King Illustrator Award Honor Book. 32 pp. ISBN 0-06-443439-7. RL=E

In this superb collection of finely illustrated work, Thomas includes poems about family, traditions, self-esteem, love, and the joy of life. The poems are inspirational and beautiful. Floyd Cooper's illustrations enhance the images and emotions found in the poems.

Turcotte, Mark. (1995). *Songs of Our Ancestors. Poems about Native Americans*. Illustrated by Kathleen S. Presnell. Chicago: Children's Press, Inc. (PB). Poetry. Native American. 48 pp. Series: *Many Voices, One Song*. ISBN 0-516-45154-5. RL=M

Turcotte, an Ojibway, introduces this collection by saying that this collection of poem-songs comes from the Native American tradition of storytelling. The stories told through the poems in this book focus on Native American heroes, heroines, history, and the struggle against the oppression brought about by the Euro-Americans as they clashed with Native American people and cultures. "The Iroquois Confederacy," "The Trail of Tears," "Wounded Knee," "Ishi," and "Chief Joseph" are all part of the powerful, overall story woven by this poet storyteller throughout these poems. The cultural and historical information in these poems highlights the perspective of Native Americans as it is related to U.S. history and culture. A glossary of terms is included.

Folklore Anthologies

Bruchac, Joseph. (1990). *Return of the Sun: Native American Tales From the Northeast Woodlands*. Illustrations by Gary Carpenter. Freedom, CA: The Crossing Press. (PB). Folklore. Native American. 208 pp. ISBN 0-89594-343-3. RL=M

In his introduction to this superb collection of twenty-seven Native American tales, Bruchac notes that there are no newly recorded tales here, because he respects the tradition among many Native American storytellers to allow stories not yet written down to remain part of the oral tradition. He includes a retelling of the Walum Olum, an epic poem from the Lenape, which was recorded in pictographs painted on wooden sticks or carved into birchbark. The Walum Olum survived the arrival of the Europeans due to the transcription and translation work of the European scholar, Constantine Samuel Rafinesque. Bruchac's process of retelling these tales includes consulting versions in the original language whenever possible and retranslating those tales. However, all the tales, with the exception of the Walum Olum, are connected to the oral tradition of storytelling, which has continued to be part of Native American life. Many of these stories highlight respect for nature, practicing peace toward each other, and appreciating the gift of life.

Cole, Joanna (Ed.). (1982). *Best-loved Folktales of the World*. Illustrated by Jill Karla Schwarz. New York: Anchor Press Doubleday. (PB). Folklore. Global. 792 pp. ISBN 0-385-18949-4. RL=M

This is an anthology of two hundred folktales from all over the world. The tales are grouped geographically in the table of contents as tales from West Europe, the British Isles, Scandinavia/Northern Europe, East Europe, the Middle East, Asia, the Pacific, Africa, North America, the Caribbean/West Indies, and Central/South America. There are 106 tales from the European continent, while 94 tales come from the rest of the world. The tales are also identified specifically by the country, culture, or region from which they originated. In the North American section, the majority of tales are from people with non-European roots, such as Native Americans and African Americans. The book includes two useful indexes at the end. The first index categorizes the tales thematically according to content. A second index of titles is also included for ease in finding a specific title. Overall, this would be a useful resource of global folktales.

Hamilton, Virginia. (1988). *In the Beginning: Creation Stories From Around the World*. Illustrated by Barry Moser. San Diego: Harcourt Brace Jovanovich. (HB). San Diego: Harcourt Brace Jovanovich, 1991. (PB). Folklore. Global. 161 pp. ISBN 0-152-38742-0. RL=D

This collection includes twenty-five creation stories from all around the globe. In her introduction, Hamilton notes that such stories are truth to those who live by them and myths to those outside the culture from which they originate. The stories are accompanied by an author's comment that gives the reader further information about the story, the culture, or both. Barry Moser's stunning illustrations add even greater depth to these well-told stories. A list of useful sources is provided at the end.

Hamilton, Virginia. (1985). *The People Could Fly: American Black Folktales.* Illustrated by Leo and Diane Dillon. New York: Alfred A. Knopf, Inc. (HB). New York: Scholastic, 1994. (PB). Folklore. African American. 178 pp. Coretta Scott King Award. ISBN 0-590-48211-4. RL=M

In her introduction to this stunning collection of twenty-four African American folktales, Hamilton writes of the historical context within which these tales were told by slave storytellers during the long years of legalized slavery in the United States. The folktales are divided into four groups, representing the main body of African American folktales. These divisions are: Animal Tales; Tales of the Real, Extravagant, and Fanciful; Tales of the Supernatural; and Slave Tales of Freedom. Hamilton feels that these tales "belong to all of us. They are part of our American tradition and part of the history of our country" (p. xii).

McKissack, Patricia C. (1992). *The Dark-Thirty: Southern Tales of the Supernatural.* Illustrated by Brian Pinkney. New York: Alfred A. Knopf, Inc. (HB). New York: Scholastic, Inc., 1993. (PB). Folklore. African American. 127 pp. Newbery Honor Award. ISBN 0-590-47735-8. RL=D

The author explains that this collection of ten suspenseful, scary, and spine-tingling stories is grounded in African American history and the tradition of oral storytelling. These are stories that the author heard as a child from her own grandmother.

McLain, Gary. (1990). *The Indian Way: Learning to Communicate With Mother Earth.* Santa Fe, NM: John Muir Publications. (PB). Short Stories/Customs/Beliefs/Folkways. Native American/Northern Arapahoe. 103 pp. ISBN 0-945465-73-4. RL=M

The author introduces his grandfather, Grandpa Iron, who was a Northern Arapahoe Medicine Man. Through his full moon stories, Grandpa Iron taught his grandchildren how people "fit into the whole of all living things" (Introduction, p. I). McLain chooses thirteen of these full moon stories to include in this book. In the second section of the book, the author includes activities based on the full moon stories to encourage understanding of the Indian way of life through hands-on experiences connected to art, dance, nature, games, and more.

Phelps, Ethel Johnston. (1981). *The Maid of the North: Feminist Folk Tales From Around the World.* New York: Holt, Rinehart and Winston. (HB).

New York: Owl Book Edition, a division of Holt, Rinehart and Winston, 1982. (PB). Folktales/Feminist. Global. 174 pp. ISBN 0-03-062374-X. RL=D

This collection of twenty-one folktales represents many different cultures around the globe. All of the tales were chosen because each tale in some way features women as heroic, intelligent, courageous characters rather than in the more typical roles of docile maidens in distress or evil ogres. There is good representation of the diversity of cultures within the collection.

Yep, Laurence. (1989). *The Rainbow People.* New York: HarperCollins. (HB). New York: HarperTrophy, 1992. (PB). Folklore. Chinese/Chinese American. 194 pp. ISBN 0-06-440441-2. RL=M

The author retells twenty powerful tales gathered from sixty-nine tales collected and translated by Jon Lee as part of the WPA Federal Writers' Project in the 1930s in Chinatown in Oakland, California. These stories had been passed down from the old-timers, Chinese men who came to America in the latter half of the nineteenth century but were unable to bring their families with them. The roots of these immigrants and their stories can be traced back to "less than a dozen counties in Kwangtung province in China" (p. xi). The tales are grouped into five categories: Tricksters, Fools, Virtues and Vices, Chinese America, and Love. These stories were carried by immigrants into their new life and helped them cross the cultural borders of the new life by maintaining a connection to their past.

Yolen, Jane. (Ed.). (1986). *Favorite Folktales From Around the World.* New York: Random House, Inc. (HB). New York: Pantheon Books, a division of Random House, Inc. (PB). Folklore. Global. ISBN 0-394-75188-4. RL=M

In this collection of 154 tales, Yolen offers the tales that are her personal favorites (p. 13). The tales are categorized by content. The tales reflect the wide diversity of human experiences and cultures. In the introduction, Yolen writes a powerful, erudite essay about the place and power of stories within and across cultures. This would be a good companion volume for the Cole (1982) collection, because Yolen deliberately chooses to include less well-known tales.

Chapter 5

Inner Borders

The works cited in this section generally include two genres of literature: (1) contemporary realistic fiction and (2) historical fiction. When the time in which a story is set is fifty or more years earlier than the present, it is considered historical fiction. In all of these works, one or more of the main characters cross borders within themselves and overcome some form of negativity or obstacle within themselves such as fear, jealousy, low self-esteem, or prejudice. The crossing of this inner border leads the characters to a new understanding about themselves and/or to greater wisdom about others and the world about them.

The works have been grouped in three thematic categories: (1) Friends and Families, (2) Courage and Survival, (3) War and Peace, and (4) Perspectives on Prejudice. Values such as love, loyalty, courage, and adaptation to change are often embedded in these stories. In some cases, a book could have been placed in more than one category.

Friends and Families

Avi. (1994). *The Barn*. New York: Orchard Books. (HB). New York: Avon Books, 1996. (PB). Novel. Historical Fiction. Euro-American. 105 pp. ISBN 0-380-72562-2. RL=E

It is 1855 in the Willamette Valley, Oregon Territory when nine-year-old Ben's father has a stroke while plowing. Ben comes home from school to help his brother and sister care for their father, who is now bedridden and completely dependent on others. Their mother had died the previous year, so now the three siblings have to work the farm to keep their homestead claim. Ben decides that he and his older siblings should work together and build a barn, because their father had always wanted to build a barn. It will be their gift to their father. While building the barn, they cope with physical and mental challenges. When the barn is done, their father dies, but he dies knowing it had been built. The story ends with the barn standing seventy years later fine and strong, and for Ben, still "something fine to come home to" (p. 106).

Boyd, Candy Dawson. (1993). *Chevrolet Saturdays.* New York: Macmillan Publishing Co. (HB). New York: Puffin Books, 1995. (PB). Novel. Contemporary Realistic Fiction. African American. 182 pp. ISBN 0-14-036859-0. RL=M

Joey Davis is confused and depressed by his parents' divorce. He is intelligent, but is having a difficult time in his fifth grade class. His teacher doesn't recognize his abilities, he is victimized by the class bully, and his mother has remarried. He has a new stepfather, Mr. Johnson. Despite Mr. Johnson's patience and kindness, Joey resists accepting him as part of his family. Joey wants his "real" family back. Events occur that force Joey to re-evaluate himself and his definition of family.

Burgess, Barbara Hood. (1991). *Oren Bell.* New York: Delacorte Press. (HB). New York: Dell Publishing, a division of Bantam Doubleday Dell Publishing Group, 1993. (PB). Novel. Contemporary Realistic Fiction. African American. 182 pp. ISBN 0-440-40747-8. RL=M

Oren Bell and his twin sister Latonya are in seventh grade. Their little sister Brenda, who is characterized as a number genius, is eight. They live with their mother, aunt and cousins, and sometimes their grandfather in a condemned house in Detroit. The slice of life depicted through the events of these children's lives is vivid. Strong, complex characterization of all the children brings the story to life. Oren has many superstitions and fears connected to the abandoned house next door. However, he acts bravely despite his fears when his grandfather and his little sister are in trouble and need him.

Dorris, Michael. (1994). *Guests.* New York: Scholastic, Inc. (PB). Novel. Historical Fiction. Native American. 119 pp. ISBN 590-73896-8. RL=E

Moss, a Native American boy, is discontented. He wants to go on his away time, so he will be treated as a man, not a boy, though everyone says it is too soon. He doesn't want to welcome the guests who are coming to his people's annual harvest feast. This is a special time for his people and his family, and he doesn't want strangers to ruin it. Against tradition, he goes away into the woods without telling anyone or taking any supplies. He panics. Then, he has an awakening experience and he meets his friend Trouble, who has also run away, because her father hits her and she refuses to behave like a girl/woman should. The two friends return to the village together to find the feast in progress and the guests telling stories, which are not totally understood because they do not speak each other's language. The view of the Europeans at the feast as seen through Moss's eyes is compelling.

Dorris, Michael. (1992). *Morning Girl*. New York: Hyperion Books. (HB). New York: The Trumpet Club, Bantam Doubleday Dell Publishing Group, 1994. (PB). Novel. Historical Fiction. Native American. 74 pp. ISBN 0-440-83359-0. Scott O'Dell Award for Historical Fiction. RL=E

This story is set in the Caribbean on the eve of Columbus's arrival from Europe. Its main characters are twelve-year-old Morning Girl and her younger brother Star Boy. In alternating chapters, Dorris writes from the point of view of each character and vividly creates a portrait of their lives that is enriched by the complexities of family relations, particularly the relationship of brother and sister. This story helps the reader cross the borders of the past and enter into the world of a pre-Columbian Caribbean people. The ending of the book portrays the arrival of the Europeans and has a haunting quality of impending disaster, which is unseen by the innocent Morning Girl who welcomes the strangers to her world.

Hamilton, Virginia. (1990). *Cousins*. New York: Philomel Books. (HB). New York: Scholastic, Inc., 1991. (PB). Novel. Contemporary Realistic Fiction. African American. 128 pp. ISBN 0-590-45436-6. RL=M

Cammy loves her family, but she is jealous of her cousin Patty Ann who seems too perfect to be real. One day the girls and several others go on a bus to a day camp together. Again, Cammy is jealous of Patty Ann because Patty Ann is relating to Elodie, who is one of Cammy's friends. Later that day, the campers are led on a hike by a counselor down to the rain-swollen Little River. The Bluety is a particularly dangerous whirlpool section. At the river, Elodie foolishly wades into the river and is in danger of being swept away. Patty Ann braves the river to rescue Elodie. Cammy watches in pride and then horror as her cousin Patty Ann succeeds in rescuing Elodie but then is sucked into the Bluety and drowned. In the weeks following Patty Ann's death, Cammy struggles with her feelings of guilt about her jealousy of Patty Ann. Eventually, Elodie and Cammy's grandmother help Cammy cross the border between guilt and forgiveness of herself.

Mathis, Sharon Bell. (1975). *The Hundred Penny Box*. Illustrated by Leo & Diane Dillon. New York: Viking Press. (HB). New York: Puffin Books, 1986. (PB). Novella. Contemporary Realistic Fiction. African American. 48 pp. Newbery Honor Book. ISBN 0-14-032169-1. RL=E

Michael's great-great Aunt Dew is a hundred years old. She has come to stay with Michael's family. She brings her old, scarred hundred penny box with her. This box contains a penny for each year of her life. Each penny represents a story and Michael wants to hear the stories. Ruth, Michael's mother, wants to get Aunt Dew a new box for her pennies, even though Aunt Dew wants to keep her old box. Michael becomes the protector of the box and advocate for Aunt Dew with his mother, who in the end, allows the hundred penny box to remain in Aunt Dew's room. This is a cross-generational story about the power of family stories to connect one generation to another.

Myers, Walter Dean. (1988). *Me, Mop, and the Moondance Kid*. New York: Delacorte Press. (HB). New York: Dell Publishing a division of Bantam Doubleday Dell Publishing Group, Inc., 1991. (PB). Novel. Contemporary Realistic Fiction. African American. Euro-American. 160 pp. ISBN 0-440-40396-0. RL=M

Mop stands for Miss Olivia Parrish. T.J. and Moondance are brothers. Mop, T.J., and Moondance grow up together in the same orphanage. Mop is Euro-American and T.J. and Moondance are African American. Now, a change has occurred, because the two brothers have been adopted and are trying to adjust to their new "family." Mop is still living at the orphanage. As she sees it, her only hope of adoption is if the coach of their baseball team, the Elks, decides to adopt her. Baseball and friendship are central to this story. Mop and the boys work together for the good of their team and their friendship grows. In the end, Marla (the coach) and her husband adopt Mop, and T.J. and Moondance adjust to their new family.

The sequel to this book is *Mop, Moondance, and the Nagasaki Knights* (ISBN 0-440-40914-4), which continues the story of Mop, T.J., and Moondance. Again, friendship and baseball are central to the story, but there is the added element of meeting and competing with baseball players from other countries, which textures the story with issues of language communication and recognition of others' needs and cultural history. Through the story of these children's lives many opportunities for discussion of cross-cultural issues may arise.

Namioka, Lensey. (1992). *Yang the Youngest and His Terrible Ear*. Boston: Little, Brown & Co., Inc. (HB). New York: Dell Publishing, a division of

Bantam Doubleday Dell Publishing Group, Inc., 1994. (PB). Novel. Contemporary Realistic Fiction. Chinese. Euro-American. 134 pp. ISBN 0-440-40917. RL=M

Yingtao Yang and his family move from China to Seattle. Everyone in the family is musically talented, except Yingtao, the youngest Yang. He starts school and makes a new friend, Matthew Connor. Matthew is a talented young violinist, but his family doesn't appreciate his musical interest. When Yingtao has to play in an important family recital, so that father can get more music students, he and Matthew create a ruse so that the audience will think Yingtao is playing and the quartet sounds wonderful. Actually, Matthew is behind a screen playing, and Yingtao is pretending to play. At the end, Matthew is able to study with Yingtao's father, and Yingtao is released from having to play the violin anymore. Instead, he is free to study and play baseball, which he loves. This is a warm and moving story about two boys from different cultures who form a friendship and help each other's talents be recognized by their families.

In the sequel, *Yang the Third and Her Impossible Family* (ISBN 0-440-41231-5), Yingmei, the sister of Fourth Brother, is the main character. Her inner struggle as an immigrant child in the United States and her desperate desire to be accepted by the other children are central to the story. When Yingmei's family is invited to share Thanksgiving dinner with the Euro-American Conner family, the difficulties of communication that occur when people know little about each other's cultural customs become apparent. Throughout the story, Yingmei seeks acceptance for herself in school with the other students. Eventually, Yingmei develops a friendship with a girl named Kim, with whom she is able to be honest and have meaningful communication. At many points in the story, Yingmei is dismayed and ashamed of her family's, particularly her mother's, inability to understand English and American ways, but in the end, she develops more understanding of her family and comes to appreciate them.

Yarbrough, Camille. (1989). *The Shimmershine Queens*. New York: G.P. Putnam's Sons. (HB). New York: Alfred A. Knopf, Inc., a Bullseye Books edition, 1990. (PB). Novel. Contemporary Realistic Fiction. African American. 142 pp. ISBN 0-679-80147-2. RL=M

Ten-year-old Angie feels depressed. She is teased by other children because of her African looks. The only time she feels good is when she spins her daydreams. Her ninety-year-old Cousin Seatta comes to visit, and gives Angie the gift of her history through telling her stories connected to the family's past and the past of her people not told in history books. They discussed the "get-up gift," dreams of courage and motivation for people to be their best. Cousin Seatta tells Angie that she has the "get-up gift" inside her. They discuss the shimmershine, the glow of self-respect, that comes from implementing the "get-up gift." After that, Angie and her best friend Michele work together to make their lives better by using their "get-up gift." They begin to study harder than ever, because they are inspired to have a lasting shimmershine which, according to Cousin Seatta, can be gained through knowledge. In this triumphant, inspirational story, Angie grows in self-respect as she applies herself to study and learn.

Yep, Laurence. (1977). *Child of the Owl*. New York: HarperCollins Children's Books. (HB). New York: Harper Trophy, a division of HarperCollins Children's Books, 1990. (PB). Novel. Contemporary Realistic Fiction. Chinese American. 217 pp. ISBN 0-064-40336-X. RL=D

Twelve-year-old Casey lives alone with her father Barney, an addicted gambler, because her mother died when she was young. Casey doesn't remember her. At the beginning of the story, Barney is beaten up and lands in a hospital, because he owes money to a bookie. Barney asks Casey's uncle (her mother's brother) to take care of Casey, but it doesn't work out, and instead Casey winds up living with her maternal grandmother, called Paw-Paw, in San Francisco's Chinatown. For the first time in her life, Casey, who has only thought of herself as American, begins to learn what it means to be Chinese as well. Through Paw-Paw, she learns about the mother she never knew and she learns about being a child of the Owl Spirit and their family's Owl Spirit's jade charm. Barney's gambling addiction causes him to steal the jade owl charm from his mother-in-law and when that theft is revealed, it causes a rift between Casey and her father. Eventually, Paw-Paw regains the charm and sells it to a museum in order to help Barney pay his gambling debts and have a bit more financial independence for herself. Through all this, Casey learns that the Owl Spirit is greater than the charm itself. She decides to remain with her grandmother. There is the beginning of a reconciliation between Casey and her father at the end, as Barney begins attending Gamblers Anonymous in an effort to change his life.

In the sequel to this book entitled *Thief of Hearts* (ISBN 0-590-97787-3), Casey's daughter Stacy is the main character. Stacy is forced to think about her Chinese American heritage when she is paired at school with Hong Ch'un, a girl newly arrived from China. This sequel is a satisfying continuation of a fascinating story.

Courage and Survival

Dorris, Michael. (1996). *Sees Behind Trees*. New York: Hyperion Books for Children. (HB). New York: Scholastic Inc., 1997. (PB). Novel. Historical Fiction. Native American. 104 pp. ISBN 0-590-10851-4. RL=M

Because he is extremely nearsighted, Walnut is unable to learn the traditional method of shooting a bow and arrow, which is required for the adult naming ceremony. So, his mother teaches him to use all his other senses to earn his adult name Sees Behind Trees. Ever since then people consult him about finding lost objects. Gray Fire, an elder of the tribe, wants to find a beautiful, mysterious place he had known as a youth. Sees Behind Trees goes on a difficult and dangerous journey with Gray Fire to find this place. They meet strangers along the way. Gray Fire dies after they come to the place they have been seeking. Sees Behind Trees learns much about himself and life before he returns to his village.

Fox, Paula. (1991). *Monkey Island*. New York: Orchard Books. (HB). New York: Dell Publishing, a division of Bantam Doubleday Dell Publishing Group, Inc., 1993. (PB). Novel. Contemporary Realistic Fiction. Euro-American and African American/Homeless. 160 pp. ISBN 0440-82408-7. RL=D

Eleven-year-old Euro-American Clay Garrity finds himself alone on the streets of New York City when his pregnant mother disappears from the low-rent residential hotel where they have been living since his father left them. Clay is befriended by Calvin and Buddy, two homeless men, who help him learn how to survive as a homeless person on the streets of New York with winter approaching. Calvin is older, Euro-American, and an alcoholic. Buddy is in his late teens and African American. Clay faces fear and despair with courage. When Clay gets sick with pneumonia, Buddy saves Clay's life by getting him to a hospital. Calvin dies during the winter. Buddy spends the winter in a shelter and gets a second chance at life. After the hospital, Clay spends time with a foster family and is then reunited with his mother and new baby sister. Clay is understandably bitter toward his mother and struggles with forgiveness and healing. He searches for Buddy until one day fate places them together again. They share their stories about what had happened to them. Buddy reminds Clay that he is one of the lucky ones. Clay reflects on everything and returns to the new home he shares with his mother and sister lighter of heart, ready to meet his new life.

George, Jean Craighead. (1972). *Julie of the Wolves*. Illustrated by John Schoenherr. New York: Harper & Row Publishers. (HB). New York:

HarperCollins Children's Books, 1972. (PB). Novel. Contemporary Realistic Fiction. Native American/Eskimo. Newbery Award. 170 pp. ISBN 0-064-40058-1. RL=D

This story is told in three parts. In the first part, Miyax (Julie) is out in the wilderness surviving with the help of the wolf pack that has adopted her. The second part is a flashback in which the events of her life that led up to her being alone in the wilderness are recounted. The third part of the story picks up where the first part stops and continues the story to completion. In the third part, Miyax endures the violent death of the wolf pack leader, her beloved Amaroq. She also nurses her wolf friend Kapu back to health after he is shot, and eventually, she finds her way back to her father Kapugen, who has remarried a Euro-American and has started a new life. This story is filled with cultural details supplied by the author's research. This is a compelling story of courage. Miyax crosses borders within herself in order to connect with another species, the wolves, and be accepted by that species as one of them.

In the superb sequel, *Julie* (ISBN 0-06-440573-7), Miyax becomes Julie once again as she works to adapt to the new way of life she finds herself living with Kapugen and his Euro-American wife Ellen. This book was written in response to thousands of children who wrote to the author wanting to know what happened to Julie after she left the wolves. The richness of the details of setting and culture that are derived from the author's research, including many visits to Alaska, are naturally woven into the story and enhance the reality of who the characters are and what happens in the plot.

Hamilton, Virginia. (1983). *Willie Bea and the Time the Martians Landed*. New York: Macmillan Publishing Company. (HB). New York: Aladdin Books, 1989. (PB). Novel. Historical Fiction. African American. 209 pp. ISBN 0-689-71328-2. RL=M

This story is based on the idea of what could have happened in an African American family in rural Ohio when "War of the Worlds" was broadcast over the radio by Orson Welles in 1938. Millions of Americans thought a real event was being reported and that they were being invaded by Martians. Willie Bea is an imaginative and courageous young girl who, despite her fear, goes out with her friend Toughy Clay to meet the aliens she believes have come to her community. She is convinced they are from Venus, not Mars. Willie Bea and Toughy Clay make their way in the dark to the farm where it is rumored the aliens have landed. The lights and noise they encounter turn out to be harvesting combines working at night, not aliens. The last chapters bring explanations and understanding of what has happened to all. This story is rich in cultural details of setting and character that greatly enhance the story.

Hill, Kirkpatrick. (1990). *Toughboy and Sister.* New York: Viking Penguin. (HB). New York: The Trumpet Club, 1992. (PB). Novel. Survival Fiction. Native American/Athabascan. 121 pp. ISBN 0-440-84915-2. RL=M

Eleven-year-old Toughboy and his little sister called "Sister" by everyone find themselves abandoned by their father at their family's fish camp on the Yukon River. Their mother had died a few weeks earlier in childbirth. Toughboy and Sister spend the summer at the fish camp surviving on their own. They face fear, loneliness, hunger, and despair together, and they help each other survive until the fall when Natasha, one of the head women at the village, comes to find them because they have not shown up at school. In the end, because their father hasn't been seen, Toughboy and Sister leave the fish camp with Natasha to begin a new life with her.

In the sequel entitled *Winter Camp* (ISBN 0-590-20518-8), Toughboy and Sister accompany old Natasha to the trapline at her winter camp in order to learn the Indian ways that are disappearing from their people's lives. Once again circumstances place them in a situation that threatens their survival. This is a satisfying sequel.

Mead, Alice. (1995). *Junebug.* New York: Farrar, Straus, Giroux. (HB). New York: Bantam Doubleday Dell Books for Young Readers, 1997. (PB). Novel. Contemporary Realistic Fiction. African American. 102 pp. ISBN 0-440-91275-X. RL=E

Junebug has the courage to work toward making his dreams a reality. He dreams that one day he and his family will be able to move away from the housing project where they live to a better neighborhood. He also loves the nearby harbor and the boats. He dreams that one day he will work there and take care of his mother and little sister Tasha. His world seems to be falling apart when his mother has to go to the hospital and he and Tasha are left with Aunt Jolita. But, he doesn't give up. After Mama's release from the hospital, Junebug, Tasha, and and Mama go on a ferry ride for his tenth birthday. He releases all fifty of his special bottles from his bottle collection into the bay, sending them out like prayers on waves of faith. Inside the bottles are notes about his dreams and his phone number. His faith is rewarded. He gets an opportunity to work in the boatyard at the harbor and learn to sail. Then, his mother gets a better job and the family moves across town to a better apartment. Thus, this story has a hopeful ending.

War and Peace

Coerr, Eleanor. *Mieko and the Fifth Treasure.* (1993). New York: G.P. Putnam's Sons. (HB). New York: Bantam Doubleday Dell Publishing Group Inc., 1994. (PB). Novella. Historical Fiction. Japanese. 79 pp. ISBN 0-440-40947-0. RL=E

Mieko and her family live in Nagasaki, Japan at the end of World War II. Mieko is a talented young calligrapher before the atom bomb is dropped on her city. Her teacher, Mr. Araki, explains that there are four treasures connected to the art of calligraphy: a fine sable brush, an inkstick, an inkstone, and a roll of rice paper. Mr. Araki tells Mieko that she is one of the few lucky ones to be born with the fifth treasure, which is beauty in the heart. The story opens two weeks after the bomb has been dropped. Mieko's life will never be the same again. Her writing hand has been badly burned, and she seems to have lost the fifth treasure. However, her family has survived. Because her father is a doctor, he and her mother remain in the city to help care for the injured, but they send Mieko to the countryside to her grandparents' farm to heal and return to school. While in the care of her grandparents, Mieko struggles to overcome her fears and depression. With the help of a new friend and the loving support of her grandparents, she crosses an inner border and learns that she has not lost the fifth treasure after all.

Coerr, Eleanor. (1977). *Sadako and the Thousand Paper Cranes.* Illustrated by Ronald Himler. New York: G.P. Putnam's Sons. (HB). New York: Dell Publishing, a division of Bantam Doubleday Dell Publishing Group, Inc., 1979. (PB). Novella. Fictionalized Biography/Historical context. Japanese. Aftermath of World War II. 64 pp. ISBN 0-440-47465-5. RL=M

This story is based on the life of Sadako Sasaki, who was two when the atom bomb was dropped on Hiroshima where she lived. The story opens in 1954 with Sadako excited about the upcoming races at school. She loves to run. On the day of the races, Sadako is dizzy at the end of the race. When her parents take her to the doctor, she is diagnosed with leukemia, the atom bomb disease. While she is in the hospital, her friend Chizuko comes to visit and teaches her to make a paper crane as a get well wish. There is an old story that if a sick person folds 1,000 paper cranes, the gods will make the person well. Before she died in 1955, Sadako had folded 644 paper cranes, which were buried with her. Sadako was courageous in the face of her illness, and her story has continued to touch the hearts of many.

Keehn, Sally M. (1995). *Moon of Two Dark Horses*. New York: Philomel Books, a division of The Putnam & Grosset Group. (HB). New York: Bantam Doubleday Dell Books for Young Readers, 1997. (PB). Novel. Historical Fiction. Native American. Euro-American. 218 pp. ISBN 0-440-41287-0. RL=D

This story begins in 1776. As the Revolutionary War intensifies, the British and the Americans attempt to sway the Native Americans to join their respective sides. This story is told from the point of view of Cooshmoo, a young Delaware boy who lives with his people along the Susquehana River at the New York/Pennsylvania border in the Wyoming Valley. The story is about Cooshmoo's memories of his friend Daniel, the son of a Euro-American settler, and what happened to them as the raging war tore them and their world apart. In an epilogue, Cooshmoo tells of his own death from a sniper's bullet and the revenge wreaked by his mother, Queen Esther. The author includes a historical note at the end about Queen Esther of the Delawares. The author also includes a bibliography of sources used to research the people and events of this period as a foundation for this novel.

Lowry, Lois. (1989). *Number the Stars*. Boston: Houghton Mifflin Company. (HB). New York: Dell Publishing, a division of Bantam Doubleday Dell Publishing Group, Inc., 1990. (PB). Novel. Historical Fiction. European Danish Christian and Jewish/Holocaust. 144 pp. Newbery Award. ISBN 0-440-91002-1. RL=M

In 1943, ten-year-old Annemarie Johansen and her best friend Ellen Rosen are both natives of Copenhagen, Denmark, which is occupied at that time by the Nazis. Annemarie is Christian and Ellen is Jewish. When the Nazis attempt to "relocate" the Danish Jews, the Christian Danes work together to save their countrymen. Through their concerted effort, nearly 7,000 Jews, almost the entire Jewish population of Denmark, are smuggled across the sea to neutral, unoccupied Sweden and safety. This book is a fictionalized story based on that history. Annemarie has to go on a dangerous mission in order to make the escape of the Rosen family secure. She finds courage within herself that she hadn't known was there.

Salisbury, Graham. (1994). *Under the Blood-Red Sun*. New York: Delacorte Press. (HB). New York: Bantam Doubleday Dell Books for Young Readers, 1995. (PB). Novel. Historical Fiction. Japanese American and Euro-American. 247 pp. ISBN 0-440-91055-2. RL=D

Tomi was born and lives in Honolulu, Hawaii. His parents and grandfather are Japanese immigrants to Hawaii. The story begins in September, 1941, when Tomi and his Euro-American best friend Billy and their Portuguese buddies, Mose and Rico, are involved in school, baseball, and their life together as "Rats." Then came the bombing of Pearl Harbor by Japan, on December 7, 1941, and Tomi's world disintegrates. His father, a fisherman, is arrested, detained, and eventually deported to an internment camp on the mainland. In the midst of the war's turmoil, the Rats have one final, great baseball game with the Kaka'ako Boys, in which for a brief time baseball takes precedence over everything else. Meanwhile, Tomi has been given the duty of guarding the Katana, the sword symbolizing the family's pride and strength, which has been handed down for generations. Tomi has to hide it until the war is over. The book ends with Tomi determined to survive the war, take care of his family, and do his duty. There are many aspects of loyalty explored in this book . . . loyalty to friends, family, ancestors, and country. Tomi's loyalties are constantly being tested as he crosses inner borders of courage and understanding of himself to answer these tests.

Perspectives on Prejudice

Spinelli, Jerry. (1990). *Maniac Magee*. Boston: Little, Brown, & Co., Inc. (HB). New York: HarperCollins Children's Books, 1992. (PB). Novel. Contemporary Realistic Fiction. Euro-American. African American. 184 pp. Newbery Award. ISBN 0-064-4042-42. RL=M

Euro-American Maniac Magee is born Jeffrey Lionel Magee. Orphaned at three, he goes to live with his Aunt Dot and Uncle Dan in Holidaysburg, Pennsylvania. He lives with them for eight years in a divided house where hate is the rule. One day, when he is eleven, Jeffrey can't take it anymore. Right in the middle of a school program, he leaps from the stage and starts running. He never returns. He runs for a year and winds up in the racially divided town of Two Mills, two hundred miles away. The first person he meets is Amanda Beale, an articulate, intelligent African American girl, who eventually becomes his friend. Maniac (Jeffrey) Magee's legend begins that first day when he does amazing things all about town, such as braving Finsterwald's backyard to rescue Arnold Jones and hitting the world's first frogball bunt homerun in a local Little League game. Such feats earn him the name of Maniac. As the story unfolds, Maniac gets involved with various people's lives throughout the town, both Euro-American and African American. He refuses to recognize the borders of prejudice and ignorance in Two Mills. Eventually, through Maniac's actions and relationships, the racial tensions dividing the town lessen. At the end of the story, Maniac finds a home with Amanda's family. Although the character of Maniac borders on being a mythical, fantasy hero, this book would provide an opportunity for dialogue about prejudice and racism.

Taylor, Mildred D. (1987). *The Friendship and the Gold Cadillac.* New York: Dial Books for Young Readers. (HB). New York: A Bantam Skylark Book, a division of Bantam Doubleday Dell Publishing Group, Inc., 1989. (PB). Two Novellas. Historical Fiction. African American. 88 pp. ISBN 0-553-15765-5. RL=M

These two novellas vividly portray racism and prejudice and the struggle to live with courage and dignity in the face of such evil. In *The Friendship,* the Logan children watch Mr. Tom Bee, an elder of their community, bravely go against the humiliating Southern custom that does not allow African Americans to call Euro-Americans by their first names, no matter what their personal relationships are. Mr. Tom Bee's righteous, courageous insistence by right of friendship to call Mr. John Wallace, the Euro-American store owner, by his first name John, results in Mr. Tom Bee being brutally attacked, yet it is not his attacker John who has the last word.

In *The Gold Cadillac,* Wilma's family makes a trip south from their Ohio home in their new gold Cadillac. During this trip, Wilma sees and feels the ugliness and fear bred by Southern-style segregation, but she also comes to understand the depth of love and loyalty within her own family, which helps her overcome her fear.

Taylor, Mildred D. (1990). *Mississippi Bridge.* New York: Dial Books for Young Readers. (HB). New York: Bantam Skylark Books, a division of Bantam Doubleday Dell Publishing Group, Inc., 1992. (PB). Novella. Historical Fiction. 1930s. Mississippi. Euro-American and African American. 62 pp. ISBN 0-553-15992-5. RL=D

Jeremy Simms, a Euro-American boy, is friends with Josias Williams and Stacey Logan, two African American boys. Jeremy does not adhere to the borders of prejudice that are so much a part of his world. On a gloomy, rain-soaked day at the end of winter in 1931, Jeremy is hanging out at the local general store, which also serves as the bus stop. Jeremy's African American friend Josias Williams is taking the bus to a new job. Several other local people, African American and Euro-American, board the bus. The Logan children arrive at the store to see their grandmother off on the bus, and then do an errand for her that forces them to cross the rickety old bridge over the rain-swollen river near the store. The bus driver readies the bus for departure. At the last minute, a large Euro-American family wants to board the bus. The bus driver forces all the African Americans to get off the bus. Reluctantly, they do so. Jeremy sadly sees his friend

Josias denied passage and humiliated. The bus pulls away and suddenly Jeremy sees the bus careen onto the bridge and crash into the river below. Despite the rescue attempted by Josias, Jeremy, and other men from the store, all the people on the bus die. Jeremy struggles to make sense of this terrible tragedy. The story ends with Jeremy working all day at Josias's side to retrieve the bodies. No easy answer is provided by the author. The reader, like Jeremy, must construct his/her own meaning from this story.

Taylor, Mildred D. (1976). *Roll of Thunder, Hear My Cry.* New York: Viking Penguin. (HB). New York: The Trumpet Club, 1991. (PB). Novel. Historical Fiction. 1930s. Mississippi. African American. 210 pp. Newbery Award. ISBN 0-440-84387-1. RL=D

The land is the lifeblood of the Logan family, but it takes the events of a turbulent year for Cassie to understand the importance of her family's ownership of their own land. It is a year of night riders and burnings. It is a year of seeing her brother's friendship betrayed and her own humiliation. It is a year of finding courage and strength to overcome everything through the bondedness of her family and their connection to the land. This connection to the land is what sets them apart from so many other families in the area, regardless of ethnicity. Cassie, and her brothers—Stacey, Little Man, and Christopher John—as well as the adult Logans are clear, complex, enduring, whole characters who inspire the reader to cheer for their triumph.

Taylor, Mildred D. (1975). *Song of the Trees.* New York: The Dial Press. (HB). New York: Bantam Books, a division of Bantam Doubleday Dell Publishing Group, Inc., 1979. (PB). Novella. Historical Fiction. 1930s. Mississippi. African American. 52 pp. ISBN 0-553-27587-9. RL=M

This fictional story is based on an actual event from the author's family history. The story is set in the 1930s in Mississippi. Cassie Logan's family owns their own land, which includes a stand of original growth trees. Cassie and her family love that patch of forest on their land. David Logan, Cassie's father, has to go to Louisiana to work laying track for the railroad, because times are hard and he needs the money to feed his family. While he is gone, a Euro-American businessman named Mr. Andersen intimidates Big Ma, Cassie's grandmother, into selling the trees from their patch of forest to him. Mr. Andersen's "deal" is that for $65.00 he can chop and take as much timber as he likes from the Logan land. Cassie and her older brother Stacey hear Mr. Andersen say he will cut down all the trees, so Cassie's mother sends Stacey to Louisiana on a mule to find Papa and bring him home to save the trees, if possible. There is a dramatic ending and, although some of the trees are felled, Papa arrives in time to stop the chopping of the trees. Papa stands up to Mr. Andersen, saves what remains of the trees, and demonstrates self-respect to his children.

Section III

Chapter 6

Using Literature of Diversity in the Classroom

This chapter will present three models for using literature of diversity in the fourth- through sixth-grade elementary classroom reading/language arts curriculum: (1) individualized reading, (2) thematic units, and (3) literature circles. Suggested activities connected to using the books and implementing these models are also included, but these suggestions are not to be considered a complete list of possible activities for extending students' engagement and connections with literature. Teachers are encouraged to be creative in presenting ways for students to respond to the literature of diversity they read. In addition, encouraging students to create their own projects and/or conduct research connected to their reading is also an option for extending the use of this literature in the classroom. The activities included in this chapter may be viewed as a foundation for that creativity.

Individualized Reading

Individualized reading means that every student in the class reads a different book. The essential ingredient needed to implement individualized reading is an adequate number of books to ensure that students will have choices with respect to which books each will read. With individualized reading, it is possible to have a larger number of titles of diversity being read in the classroom at one time than with other models. It is useful to organize individualized reading by taking a genre approach, highlighting such genres as contemporary realistic fiction or historical fiction.

Implementation of Individualized Reading

Introduce the focus genre to the students by giving book talks about several titles that demonstrate the characteristics of that genre. Generally, have as many books as possible connected to the genre in the classroom. If the school has a library and a librarian, enlist the help of the librarian to bring titles of diversity from the school library to supplement your classroom library collection. Consult the genre appendix in this book.

The teacher needs to set a date by which students should have their choices approved by the teacher and by which they must begin reading their books. Also set a date that will allow a reasonable amount of time to finish the books (i.e., two to four weeks). Plan blocks of time for silent sustained reading (SSR) of the books in class. If regular homework is standard school policy, include reading time as part of the homework, but remind students that they must bring the books to school every day in order to participate in SSR at school. If homework is not a school policy or the teacher prefers to keep the books in the classroom, more reading time in class may be needed and/or perhaps an extension of the overall reading time for completion of the book will be necessary. These practical contingencies will vary among classrooms, schools, districts, states, and so on.

Journaling Activities

As students read their books, they may keep a journal. Small standard composition books with twenty or forty pages are quite useful for this activity, but journals may also be constructed using binder paper inside a construction paper cover bound with staples. Students may write in their journals after they have finished reading each chapter. See Figure 6.1 for suggested types of journal entry activities.

Journal activities may be assigned for the whole class. For instance, students might all record descriptive sentences that they noticed while reading a chapter in their books. Or, a list of journal activities such as in Figure 6.1 can be given to the students, who are then allowed to choose a different journal activity for each chapter of their book until the list is exhausted; then they can repeat activities. Another option is to generate a list of journal options with students in a whole class lesson. If students have not had experience with journal activities, it is best to have direct teaching lessons about such activities during reading instruction time in the classroom. The journals may be evaluated by the teacher as students progress through their books, as well as upon completion of the books.

Figure 6.1. Suggested Journal Entry Activities

1. new vocabulary
2. similes/metaphors
3. descriptive passages
4. dialogue that enhances the plot
5. predicting questions
6. character descriptions
7. personal responses/opinions
8. poems based on characters, events, or themes
9. illustrating actual characters or scenes
10. imaginative sketches based on the story (i.e., drawing a character from the story in a setting that shows a place the student has visited that is not in the story)
11. diary entries of a character
12. letters from one character to another
13. a cartoon strip of the events of the chapter

Student Sample. Newspaper Article

Greg Hits Winning 3-Run Home Run

By David Halperin

Last year the Elks won the championship game against the Eagles, and they have done it again! It was all done with the help of a player named Greg. He hit a 3-run home run over the outfield wall. He used to live in the woods but then he was put in a shelter. A couple other times Greg was the hero of baseball games. But his 3-run home run was the best.

After Greg hit the home run, all the players were jumping around with joy. Greg felt really happy for himself and the team. It was just great for the Elks to defeat the Eagles again. With Greg's help, the Elks have become more famous.

Inspired by: _Mop, Moondance, and the Nagasaki Knights_ by Walter Dean Myers.

Student Sample. Variety Letter

Letter From Student to Book Character

By Lauren Moy

Dear Mop,

How are you? I'm fine. How old are you? I'm eight. I heard that you got in the champions. Great! How come you thought Marla wasn't going to adopt you? You should've thought, "Maybe Marla will adopt me, and I don't think I need T.J.'s help either." Anyway, I heard about Taffy. She sounded like a nice animal to have. I'm sorry that she had to go. I don't like it when you threaten people. Don't tackle people, because you are mean when you do that. I find it very rude. Well, you are a good friend to T.J. and you both are very lucky to have each other. I have a friend like that too.

Love,
Lauren Moy

Inspired by: Me, Mop, and the Moondance Kid by Walter Dean Myers

---

Student Sample. Newspaper Article

Arrows Scared Out of Their Skins!

By Mattias Lehman

There was excitement last night in a small foggy area one mile from town near a forest. Thomas Small, Professor Small, and Pesty, along with Mr. Pluto and his son scared the Darrows out of their skins.

It all started when the Small family came to live in the old Dies Drear House. There was no electricity. They used candles to light the house. They used a wood stove for cooking their meals.

Mr. Pluto and his son were there. Pesty was on a horse. Thomas Small and Professor Small wore chains and metal pieces. They were all coated with phosphorescent paint. Then they walked moaning and groaning toward the Darrows. The Darrows went running as fast as possible down the path with their hands stretched out, hair on edge, and they have never been seen again.

Inspired by: The House of Dies Drear by Virginia Hamilton

Culmination Response Activities

When the books are completed, it enhances the sense of being a community of readers in the classroom to have a class culmination response activity based on the books. There are a variety of options for such activities. These may be visual art projects, written activities, drama/oral activities, or any combination of these.

Visual Art A variety of media may be used, such as different papers, markers, crayons, colored pencils, and different paints (tempera, water color, or acrylic) to create visual art projects. With all visual art projects, encourage students to use the entire space provided on the paper for their composition. (I tell my students that one of my favorite words with respect to their drafts is "bigger.") Talk to students about the necessity of doing more than one draft in the planning of a project. Explain that artists, like writers, do drafts of work before finalizing a project. Insist on completely colored backgrounds. Look at art prints and/or illustrations in books and talk about the way the artists use line, space, color, texture, and form. If available, computer art programs may also be used to create visual art projects. Bulletin board displays are frequently a fact of life in fourth- through sixth-grade classrooms. Mounted visual art accompanied by some form of mounted writing can make a stunning "Literature of Diversity" bulletin board to highlight and display the creative responses and thoughtful connections students have made to this literature.

Sample Projects

Create a Bookmark 3" × 10" pieces of oak or white tagboard make wonderful size bookmarks. Cut blank newsprint to the same size, so that students can draft their bookmarks. I instruct them to include title, author, and illustrator if there is one. Plan the lettering first. Then create a picture that either shows one or more characters or an artifact that is central to the story. A poem may be written to accompany the bookmark.

Create a 3-D Poster Use oak or white tagboard cut to 8½" × 11½" to create this variation of the standard book poster. (Using this size makes the finished product easy to mount by backing it with a 9" × 12" piece of construction paper.) Cut blank newsprint the same size and have students design the setting. They need to include the title and author of the book in the design. They then transfer their design to the tagboard. Then, students use pieces of tagboard to create the characters who go into the setting. Use short (about 1 inch) accordion-folded backings glued to the characters to attach the characters to the setting. Use as many of these backings as necessary to secure the characters. Attaching the characters in this way gives a three-dimensional effect to the poster. A written book review may accompany the poster.

Book Jacket Use a sheet of 12" × 18" white drawing paper folded in half as the basic form to create a book jacket. If desired, front and back flaps can be created by folding the sides three inches toward the inside of the paper. Students decide on an important scene from their books and then illustrate it on the jackets. They need to incorporate the title, author, and illustrator (if there is one) into the design of the book jacket. Use 12" × 18" blank newsprint for drafting designs. A written summary of the story may be written on the jacket flaps or stapled inside the book jacket.

Draw a Character Whatever size drawing paper is used, have blank newsprint cut to that size for planning drafts. Have students fold the newsprint draft paper into thirds. Explain that the character they draw should be visualized in thirds and that each third of the character fills a third of the paper. That way, students will compose larger characters, which will be more visually appealing, especially for display. Have them outline their characters with a dark marker or crayon. Generally children are more likely to become discouraged with visual art when they are looking at something and their own picture doesn't look to them like the picture at which they are looking. Therefore, it is advisable not to have them look at a picture of a character in a book as they sketch their draft. Tell them to imagine the character and whatever their style is, that is their unique, wonderful depiction of the character. This project is an excellent opportunity to use illustrated books to show a wide variety of artists' styles in order to validate the concept of artistic variation.

Written Response Activities Final writing activities may or may not be ideas that originated from journal activities engaged in by students as they read the books. Here are some suggested writing activities that have worked well with many fourth- through sixth-grade students.

1. Write a Poem

   Poems may be free verse or a particular structure or pattern that has been presented in class previously.

2. Write a Reader's Theatre Script

   Create a script based on an important chapter in the book.

3. Pitch an Idea

   Write a paragraph or more proposing an idea for a sequel or prequel to the book.

4. Write a Book Review

   Write a book review that includes a brief summary of the book, as well as your opinion and recommendation to future readers about this book.

Student Samples. Poems

The Shimmershine Feeling

By Ashley Norwood

The Shimmershine Feeling
Makes my heart glow
It makes me think of special things
Sometimes my thoughts show
When I have the Shimmershine Feeling
It's like bells ringing ting-aling-ding
The Shimmershine Feeling
Doesn't sound very enchanting
But when you have that certain feeling
The thoughts are very appealing.

Inspired by: _The Shimmershine Queens_ by Camille Yarbrough

The Feeling of Guilt

By Taylor Heisley-Cook

I feel so guilty
Cause my cousin died,
I feel so guilty
She was just
Within a stride
Of me reaching her
Even though she saved another
She was my friend
I feel so guilty
Cause my cousin died.

Inspired by: _Cousins_ by Virginia Hamilton

Student Samples. Poems

Song for Amaroque By Danielle Amerian	**Jobs** By Alison Lisnow
Oh my dear Amaroque Even in death You are still my adopted father And will always be. You rise to my heart As I hear your spirit voice Inside my gloomy soul. Oh, my loving Amaroque How I miss you so At night I always cry myself to sleep When the stars shine In the ebony sky. You live in me And you will always be my Morning star. But now, my Amaroque, Your spirit is free at last. Inspired by: <u>Julie of the Wolves</u> by Jean Craighead George	We have lots of jobs to do If you think that is easy Why don't you Try to do the jobs we do. We: Catch fish No one will buy them No matter how hard we wish. We: Scratched fleas off of 13 cats We had to use the money I'll tell you that. We did much more Find us around And more jobs We'll explore! Inspired by: <u>Boys At Work</u> by Gary Soto

Oral/Dramatic Activities Oral/dramatic activities help to bring stories to life for all. Here are some viable possibilities for such activities.

1. Storytelling

    Retell the story in the oral tradition of storytellers. This is particularly effective with folklore.

2. Meet My Favorite Character

    Students create a costume for their favorite character from the book. They prepare a two- to three-minute speech in which they tell who they are and summarize what the story is about, focusing on what happens to them in the story. This retelling is told in first person, as if they are the characters. Then, for the next three to five minutes, students from the audience question the student about the story. The presenting student must answer these questions, all the while staying in character and maintaining the character's point of view.

When used with biographies, extra research on the person can be easily included.

3. Commercial Advertisement

   Do a short (one to two minutes) radio commercial advertising the book.

4. Sing a Song

   The performer may choose to write an original song to sing or sing a popular song which is connected to the story. The singer would need to explain the connection of the song to the story prior to performing it.

5. Puppetry

   Perform a scene from the story with two or more puppets based on characters from the story. These puppets may be made using various materials and skills.

6. Book Talk Around the Room

   Students work in pairs. Students are either the A partner or the B partner. Each partner will have two to three minutes to talk to the other about the book they read. After each partner in a pair has had his/her turn, it is time for partner rotation. The A partners remain in their seats and the B partners rotate one seat to the right. The sharing process is repeated with a new partner. Rotate as many times as possible within the period. Leave time at the end to come back together as a large group and ask questions of the whole group based on the activity. See Figure 6.2 for some sample questions that could be discussed. After all this talk and discussion, it is also possible to have students write the answers to the questions in Figure 6.2 in their journals.

Figure 6.2. Whole Class Questions for Book Talk Around the Room

---
1. What book did you hear about from a classmate that you are now interested in reading?
2. What did your classmate say about a book that caught your interest? Explain.
3. Did your telling about your book change from the first person to whom you spoke to the last person?
4. Did you think of more details?
5. Did you focus on the same story events each time you told about the book?
---

7. Dance

    Students create and perform a dance based on the story. They may or may not include dialogue or song in their presentation.

8. Game Time

    Students create an interactive game based on the story. This game in some way involves other members of the class. The presenters explain the rules and teach the game to the class, and explain the ways in which the game is connected to the story.

The Teacher's Role in Individualized Reading

The teacher's role in an individualized reading program is to facilitate the time for children to browse, choose, and read books in class. Guidance is also part of the teacher's role, so it is necessary for the teacher to read many of the books in the classroom library to help students as needed with book selection. Another aspect of the teacher's role is to motivate by modeling both through enthusiastic and knowledgeable book talks and through modeling proficient reading strategies. Reading aloud combined with thinking aloud are excellent teaching strategies to use in combination in order to demonstrate a great range of proficient reading strategies. Silently reading while the students are reading is another way for a teacher to model to students that reading is important. Finally, a very important aspect of the teacher's role in an individualized reading program is conferencing with students, both informally and formally. Talking to students about books they are reading has the potential to heighten their interest, focus their thinking, and engage them more deeply in the act of reading.

Individualized reading is a flexible model for using literature in the classroom, because it accommodates a great range of reading levels and interests among students. Using the genre approach to individualized reading helps the teacher focus the lessons and enhances manageability. Individualized reading encourages self-selection of literature among students and it enables one to present a great many titles of diversity to the class in a short period of time, thus expanding the students' knowledge of titles and authors of diversity.

Thematic Units

Creating thematic units for using literature of diversity in the classroom combines various materials, activities, and content areas to teach a concept, idea, or theme. Broader themes lend themselves to more flexibility, which encourages creative and critical thinking. A thematic approach to using literature of diversity in the classroom encourages comparisons and connections to be made across genres, as well as across cultural/ethnic borders.

Into the Theme

There is a process involved in implementing a thematic literature unit. The first step is to choose an overall focus theme. When choosing a focus theme, the broader the theme, the better. For example, such focus themes as courage, tolerance, or change work well with literature of diversity. The next steps are to choose the books to be used, read the books, and then bring the books into the classroom. Once those steps are completed, it is time to present the chosen focus theme to the students.

Conduct a brainstorming session with the class. Use a large piece of paper, such as butcher paper or light-colored bulletin board paper, which can be rolled for storage and taken out later for reference as needed. Using a large marker, write the focus theme in the middle of the paper and draw a ring around it. Have students contribute all the words they can think of connected to the overall focus theme. The teacher records the contributions and creates a webbing of ideas connected to the focus theme during the brainstorming session. When students seem to have said all they can, stop the session.

Next, give brief book talks about some of the books. These book talks may include reading poems or excerpts from works, as well as simply talking about the works. As these book talks are given, ask students to listen and make connections between what they hear in the book talk and the ideas the class has just brainstormed. They may write notes on the webbing as they listen. Try to give three or more book talks at this time. Stop after each book talk and ask what connections they have noticed between that book and the overall focus theme. When all the book talks are completed, ask the students what connections they see among the books that have been presented and some aspect of the overall focus theme. They may refer to the class webbing of the focus theme created during the brainstorming session. It may be necessary to devote another class period to presenting the books to the class and discussing the connections of these books to the class's focus theme. This foundation work is important to heighten the overall confidence students later feel about making connections between the overall focus theme and the books they read.

Reading the Books

Once the overall focus theme and the books have been introduced and discussed, it is time to engage the students with reading particular works. There are various grouping options possible for reading the books depending on the availability of materials, scheduling, and so on. The following options will be presented: teacher read-aloud with or without multiple copies, partnered student reading of the same title, comparing two titles by assigning half the class one title to read and half the other title to read. It is possible to have more than one of these options functioning in the classroom at a time. Small groups will be discussed in the section on implementing literature circles.

Teacher Read-Aloud In this format, the teacher reads aloud from an overall focus theme-related novel. Students listen. Students write and/or sketch in their literature notebooks as determined by the teacher. These writings/sketchings can occur after the reading, or students may be instructed to write questions or thoughts or sketch images connected to the story as they listen. If multiple copies can be acquired, they can be used so students can read silently while the teacher reads aloud. The teacher may or may not choose to involve students in oral reading on a volunteer basis. If multiple copies are used, writing/sketching would take place after the reading. The teacher stops as needed to discuss the book. Sometimes the teacher's questions may be simple recall questions, but the most interesting discussions will be elicited by posing more open-ended questions involving application, analysis, synthesis, or evaluation. Another variation of the teacher read-aloud is for the teacher to schedule two read-aloud times in the day and read a different book connected to the theme at each time—that is, a contemporary realistic fiction book and a historical fiction book. With review discussion before each reading, students generally have no trouble following two different stories.

Partnered Student Reading Partnered reading may be used in a variety of formats. For instance, if multiple copies of the novel being read aloud are available, there may be reading sessions where students read aloud to each other as partners. During these sessions, the teacher circulates about the room listening and observing. Follow-up work connected to the reading should also be talked about and worked on together by the partners. Another way to provide students with the opportunity to work in partners is to have duplicate copies of a variety of titles, which can be distributed among partnered students. Still another permutation is to split the class in half giving each half a particular title. (They can draw random numbers 1 and 2.) Throughout the process of reading the books, students can sometimes meet with a partner who is reading the same book and sometimes meet with a partner who is reading the other book. See Figure 6.3 for questions that may be used to start students thinking about comparing and contrasting the way the books they are reading connect to the overall focus theme.

Figure 6.3. Discussion Questions for Thematic Units

> 1. How does the main character show the overall focus theme in his/her actions and/or speech?
> 2. Does the problem or problems encountered by the main character(s), as well as how those problems are handled, show some aspect of the overall focus theme? If so, in what ways?
> 3. Which events in the story seem strongly connected to the overall focus theme?
> 4. In what ways does the ending show the overall focus theme?
> 5. In what ways do you see similarities and/or differences between your life experiences and those of characters in the book?
> 6. Think about the overall focus theme. Write a life lesson message statement based on the book and connected to the overall focus theme.

Both partnered reading and teacher read-aloud formats can be used to integrate poetry, nonfiction, and folklore, as well as novels, into the exploration of the overall focus theme through literature.

Closure: Shared Response Activities

When the books have been completed, students work with a partner to present to the class how the books they read expressed the class focus theme. Students can be partnered with someone who read the same book or the other book. They can be partnered with someone they worked with previously or someone different according to teacher preferences. Here are some possible response activities students could present together to the class to share these books formally within the class.

Response Activities to Share the Books

1. A Poem for Two Voices

    Students write a poem based on the books and the theme with two parts. Then the students perform the poem together. Use *Joyful Noise* (1988) by Paul Fleischman as a model of this format.

2. Conversation

If students read different books, each student becomes a main character in the book he/she read, and the two students talk to each other as those characters about what happened to them in the stories connected to the overall focus theme. If the students read the same book, they each choose an important character and have a conversation about what happened to them in the book, focusing on how what happened connected to the focus theme.

3. Letter Writing and Reading

Students may assume the persona of a character from the book they read. They write letters to each other based on the books they read. If they read the same book, they obviously cannot be the same character. The letters should be based on the story and show how the story expresses the focus theme. Another option is for students to write letters to each other as themselves discussing the book. In ei-

Student Samples. Variety Letters

Letter to a Classmate

Dear Andrew,

I think that Yang was very nice, but his family could've treated him better. But at the end, father was very nice to Yang and that made Yang very pleased. Not forgetting Matthew and his father, Matthew was Yang's friend because he was very nice and Matthew's father liked Yang because he had a great eye.

Yang was bad at the violin and bad at batting. The results came out good, because at the end Yang hit a home run and Yang switched to the triangle, which was better for him and what he liked to do more. It doesn't say this in the book, but I would guess that he was very good at the triangle.

I think that Yang handled all his situations well.

From your friend
Marcello Tataria

Response to a Classmate's Letter

Dear Marcello,

I think you're right about how Yang's family treated him badly. But, I think it was wrong for Yang to cheat at the recital by lip syncing. At least, he found an instrument that he could play.

Sincerely,
Andrew Cha

Inspired by: Yang the Youngest and His Terrible Ear by Lensey Namioka

ther option, the presentation is to read their letters to each other in front of the class.

The Teacher's Role in Thematic Units

The teacher's role in the thematic model is one of planner and implementer, because a great deal of planning is involved to gather books and any other desired materials, as well as plan and implement integrated lessons related to various subjects connected to the overall focus theme and the literature reflecting that theme. Beyond planning and implementing, the teacher also takes on the role of observer and facilitator. For instance, when students are engaged with partnered reading, the teacher can take this opportunity to move about the room observing students reading together and listening to each other. The teacher facilitates the work of students with literature of diversity by providing them with the appropriate time, space, and discussion strategies to engage with the literature and each other cooperatively and proficiently in the classroom. As a provider of discussion strategies, the teacher engages in direct teaching that connects to particular aspects of literature (i.e., plot, theme, characters, setting, point of view) needed by the students to further their work with the books. Homework with this model is most effective when it is directly related to activities or strategies with which students have engaged in class.

Suggested thematic groupings of many of the books highlighted in Section II can be found in Appendix A. Connecting books to a general focus theme gives students the opportunity to think deeply and make connections among themselves, the world, and literature.

Literature Circles

The use of literature circles has mushroomed in classrooms since about 1990. There are excellent resources for teachers to read connected to the philosophy, rationale, and practical implementation of literature circles (Short & Pierce, 1990; Daniels, 1994; and Hill, Johnson, & Noe, 1995; Rosser & Martinez, 1995). The following discussion highlights some of the basic elements of literature circles. This is a model for engaging students with literature that offers a great deal of flexibility to the teachers and students while providing a manageable structure for teachers to empower their students. Perhaps that is the secret of success of literature circles. It is a model that has broad appeal for both students and teachers.

Definition

Basically, literature circles are small discussion groups where students meet regularly to discuss and respond to books (Daniels, 1994; Hill,

Johnson, & Noe, 1995). Some degree of self-selection of the literature to be read is a key aspect of literature circles. In most instances, it is necessary to have multiple copies (four to six) of a title to use for a literature circle. The titles presented by the teacher may be linked by theme or genre. With respect to using the books highlighted in the "Borders" chapters in this book, the appendices in this book provide suggestions for linking the titles in various ways. Once the teacher has decided upon the titles to highlight and has gathered the books needed, he/she begins by giving book talks about the books that are available for literature circles. Then, grouping can be implemented. The options for grouping presented here have been evolved in actual work with students and teacher colleagues over the last few years.

Grouping Students

Option 1. Grouping by Titles Chosen by Students Students choose the title they want to read and then the teacher divides them into groups of three or four students according to those choices. After the initial book talks, have students record three choices. The teacher tells the students that an attempt will be made to honor their first or second choice, but they should only write down books they really want to read, because such practicalities as the number of volumes available and/or the size of groups may mean that someone will be assigned their third choice. Though more than one group can read the same book, if there are sufficient copies, students are ultimately exposed to more literature when every group is reading a different book.

Option 2. Teacher Groups Students, Who Then Select Titles In this second option, the teacher divides the class into small groups of three or four students, intermingling reading ability groupings, personalities, gender, and cultural backgrounds to achieve as heterogeneous groupings as possible. After the initial book talks by the teacher and the assignment of groups, the students select the book that their group will read and discuss. Students are instructed to talk to each other about the kinds of books they like to read. The only "rule" about selection in this option is that no one in the group can have read the book previously. This restriction means they have to talk about the books available in order to make their choice.

Meetings Begin

Once the books are chosen and the groups are formed, the meetings begin. The teacher schedules two or three meeting times per week for literature circles. Meetings can begin with a brief lesson presented by the teacher.

This is especially useful in the beginning when students need guidance with respect to working cooperatively. For instance, they have to learn to set reading goals that are attainable by everyone in the group. Sometimes it is useful to give all the groups a focus question for the day's discussion, such as a question connected to an element of story, or a personal response oriented question.

Journals

Writing in journals may be a part of the work of literature circles also. These journals may be useful as a record of reading and constructing meaning throughout the process of reading and discussing the book. The journals can be collected by the teacher for evaluation at the end of a group's work with a particular book. If the journals are to be collected and graded, then students need to be told that from the beginning. Standards of legibility, mechanics, neatness, presentation, and so on need to be communicated to the students. In addition to evaluation at the end, it is useful for the teacher to randomly check the journals in a rotating fashion as the groups are meeting. In their group meetings, students decide what type of journal entry they want to do connected to each chapter. Sometimes everyone in the group can do the same type of entry and sometimes individuals in the group can do different types of entries. The key is for students to discuss these choices. There are many possibilities for journal entries, both written and artistic. See Figure 6.4 for suggested journal entry formats. Literature circle groups can also be encouraged to create their own format for journal entries. These ideas can be shared in a whole class discussion and thus add to students' knowledge of possible journal entries while simultaneously increasing the sense of the classroom as a community of learners.

Ending With Drama

Dramatic presentations offer many creative ways for the groups to share their books with the class as a whole. Such options as those listed in Figure 6.5 all work well. The complexity of these presentations will vary. Even though the teacher may limit the choices of types of performance because of time constraints and other practical contingencies, students still have many decisions to make within their groups related to material, rehearsals, and execution in order to carry out these final presentations. Rehearsals become the focus of group meetings when the need for rehearsals is reached. The day the groups perform their presentation for the class is an exciting day and greatly enjoyed by all.

Figure 6.4. Suggestions for Journal Entries

1. Design a set of clothes one of the main characters in your book might wear.
2. Pretend a character in your story is taking a trip. Where would he/she go? What would he/she pack and why?
3. Sketch an illustration for a scene in the book that is not already illustrated.
4. Pretend you could spend a day with one of the characters in the book. Which one would you choose and why?
5. Draw a sketch of the place where the main character lives.
6. Draw a comic strip for a chapter in your book. Include dialogue bubbles.
7. Write a letter from one character to another in the story that shows what happened in the chapter.
8. Write a diary entry as if you are one of the main characters. In the diary entry, show what happened in the chapter to that character.
9. Write a letter to a classmate telling them about the story so far. Be sure to include your personal thoughts/responses to the story so far.
10. Pretend you are one of the characters in the story. Who would you choose to be? Why?
11. Pretend that you can talk to one of the characters in the story. Who would you choose? Why? What would you ask? What would they answer? Write at least three questions and answers.
12. Pretend you are a newspaper reporter. You cover one of the events in the story. Now, write a headline and an article in the style of a newspaper based on that story event.
13. What was an obstacle encountered by one of the main characters in the story? How did he/she deal with that obstacle?
14. What are some items from the real world that remind you of this story? Sketch those items and write a caption telling how they remind you of the story.
15. Write a poem connected to your story. It can be a pattern poem (Haiku, cinquain, diamante, etc.) or a free verse poem.

Student Samples. Variety Letters

Letter From One Character to Another From the Same Book

Dear Abuelita,

I am having a horrible time. I miss you. First, everyone started beating me up, and then Johnny got beat up too. Then one day, Mami was coming home and the neighbors poured a freezing cold bucket of water on her. She could have had a concussion. Now we are scared of ever going outside. We went to the landlord to complain but he just told us to move. That would be difficult, because we just got here. Someone might break down the door. I hope we move back. Mami and Papi have been talking about us moving back. I'm praying it's soon. Abuelita, I wish you were here. You could make things better. Just seeing you would make me feel better during this terrible time. You answer all my questions. You make life so much easier. I miss my friend, I miss my old school, I miss my apartment, but most of all, I miss you, Abuelita.

       Love,
       Felita
       (AKA Keily Miller)

Based on: <u>Felita</u> by Nicholasa Mohr

Letter From One Character to Another From the Same Book

Dear Daddy,

 Mama told me that you are flying into Berkeley for Thanksgiving. I want to make it official that I am eating two Thanksgiving dinners this year. One dinner with you and one dinner with Mama and Mr. Johnson.

 I am glad that you got your job, and I know that you are busy, but please try to call me more.

 I am still having trouble in school. I have your new number above my phone, so that I can call you if I need to make an important decision.

       Love,
       Joey
       (AKA Kimberly Smith)

PS. I can't wait to see you on Thanksgiving.
PPS. I miss you.

Based on: <u>Chevrolet Saturdays</u> by Candy Dawson Boyd

> **Letter as the Main Character by Emily Rosenthal**
>
> Dear Mother and Father,
>
> I miss you so dearly. My feelings are great in a pot full of memories I give to you.
>
> Tomasi gave us a test yesterday. I got an A! Sala is having a marvelous time. She wishes you could come here and live with us. Poota is the best hunter on Nesak Island. What is new for you, Mother and Father?
>
> Love,
> Elizapee (Apoute)
>
> P.S. Mother, the long underwear did help.
>
> Inspired by: <u>Drifting Snow</u> by James Houston

Figure 6.5. Dramatic Performance Options

> 1. Readers' Theatre—Students choose sections from the story and create a readers' theatre script, which is then performed.
> 2. Improv Scene—Improvisational performance of one or more important scenes (no props, costumes, make up, etc.).
> 3. Skits—Performance of one or more important scenes with the addition of props, costumes, make up, etc.
> 4. Puppet Plays—Students create puppets (even simple paper bag or stick puppets are effective) and depict one or more scenes from the book.
> 5. Masked Players Tell the Story—Students create masks to represent the various characters central to the story and then tell the story as those characters wearing the masks.
> 6. Musical Theatre—Students write songs and choreograph dance numbers to interpret a scene they choose to perform.

The Teacher's Role in Literature Circles

The teacher's role in literature circles is one of guidance and facilitation. Once the students are organized with respect to the basic functioning of their literature circles, the teacher does direct teaching through whole class lessons as needed with respect to response activities, aspects of story, or reading strategies. When students are meeting in their groups, the teacher circulates around the room listening and observing student interaction about the books. The teacher may also use this time to do random, informal readings of journal entries to provide direct written or oral feedback to students.

Challenges

There are challenges that accompany the use of literature of diversity in the classroom. "Language and reality are dynamically intertwined" (Freire, 1983, p. 11). This is never more true than when a teacher chooses to make literature of diversity part of the reality of the classroom reading experiences of his/her students. Literature of diversity will challenge assumptions about ethnicity, class, gender, and power. Through nonfiction, stories, and poems, racism and prejudice will be unmasked. The worldview of students and teachers will be in a state of expansion and transformation through engaging with these books. In addition, using literature of diversity in the classroom means challenging the hegemony by broadening the traditional canon of children's literature to include authentic works of literature by and about people of color.

These challenges call for courage and commitment on the part of teachers. The teacher is the key, because the teacher is the figure of power in a classroom. Therefore, the overall stance the teacher adopts toward pluralism as a concept and the use of literature of diversity as a tangible product of that concept is important.

Many of these works of diversity will definitely raise questions about issues of power and the expression of power. Euro-American students may for the first time be in the position of seeing a Euro-American character cast in the role of villain. This may arouse feelings of guilt and/or defensiveness in those students. The teacher needs to be ready to guide students through a discussion of those feelings, and what students can learn from those feelings about themselves and the choices they may have to make connected to crossing borders. Likewise, students of color may for the first time see someone of their culture playing the role of hero or heroine in a story. Again, the teacher needs to be ready to discuss the feelings that may arise in that kind of situation. Respectful communication is a powerful tool in the classroom. Literature of diversity will offer challenges and rewards as it becomes connected with the reality of life in the classroom.

CHAPTER 7

Selecting Literature of Diversity

Literary Quality

Before a work was included in this book, it was examined with respect to literary quality. For instance, in works of fiction use of language, plot, and character development were examined. Clarity of writing to convey content, organization of material, and source documentation for authenticity of content were considered in the case of nonfiction. Poetry was examined with respect to richness of language, imagery, form, and use of poetic devices. It was counterproductive to the main purpose of this book to include a title of inferior literary quality in the annotations only because it presented a point of view of a particular culture. Literary quality was considered first, and then key issues connected to selecting literature of diversity in particular were considered.

There are basically three key issues connected to selecting literature of diversity: authenticity, bias, and balance.

Authenticity

Cultural authenticity is the primary issue in the selection of literature of diversity (Bishop, 1992; Cai & Bishop, 1994; Horning & Kruse, 1991; Howard, 1991; Kruse, 1992; Nieto, 1992; Reimer, 1992; Tway, 1989; Yokota, 1993). A book that is written from an insider's perspective is written by an author of the cultural group depicted in that book (Cai & Bishop, 1994; Kruse, 1992). Such literature represents the "experience, consciousness, and self-image developed as a result of being acculturated and socialized within those groups" (Cai & Bishop, 1994, p. 66). Culturally authentic books are true, real, genuine, verifiable, legitimate, solid, honest, tangible, and imaginable (Howard, 1991). Controversies that arise are almost always about books written by someone, usually a Euro-American, not from the cultural perspective depicted in the book in question. Although there have been some culturally authentic books written by someone outside the culture depicted, such books are the exception and are the products of gifted writers who make the effort to understand, to learn, and to inhabit another world, in order to write about it. Problematic books may misrepresent some aspects of daily life and/or culture because of ethnocentricity or bias, or even racism (Bishop, 1987). It is imperative that educators, editors in publishing houses, and book reviewers read extensively the literature of insiders in order to sensitize themselves to cultural authenticity, and thus be able to discriminate effectively among the works of literature presented as reflections of diversity (Bishop, 1992; Kruse, 1992).

Bias

Literature can serve as an effective tool to discuss stereotypes and begin to reduce prejudice. It is imperative that literature of diversity be examined for bias. Certain characteristics are key when examining literature for bias. Watch for characters of color who are treated as stereotypes in both text and illustrations. Demeaning images may be blatant or subtle. Relationships between and among characters are important. Be alert for omissions that lead to inaccuracy of portrayal. Also, remember that exclusion is a painful form of bias. Be as inclusive as possible when selecting a group of books for use with students (Day, 1994).

Accuracy and richness of detail in depicting a culture with respect to characterization, setting, plot, point of view, and theme are important in order to avoid stereotypical depiction. For instance, the language of the narrative and the dialogue are extremely important when examining a work for bias. Dialogue should never show a "character as intellectually inferior or as an object of ridicule" (Bishop, 1992, p. 51). The possible effect of a book on a child's self-image is important to consider. Imagine yourself as the child reading the book and consider whether anything in the book would embarrass or offend you if it were written about you or the group with which you identify (Day, 1994; Bishop, 1987).

Balance

When selecting literature of diversity for the classroom, a balance of various genres of literature with differing perspectives should be considered (Bishop, 1992; Norton, 1990; Yokota, 1994). The books included should also reflect diversity within and across human cultures, because this helps children to expand their worldview (Bishop, 1992). As much as possible, a balance among various literary genres is important, because then the wide spectrum of literature is present (Yokota, 1994).

While seeking balance, it is important to remember that within any particular sociocultural ethnic group, a wide range of diverse human experiences is possible, and therefore the literature one selects should reflect that diversity of experience within groups also. Generally, considerations of perspective and literary genre are both useful for achieving balance in an equitable literature curriculum (Cai & Bishop, 1994; Yokota, 1993).

Selection Tips for Teachers

Tip #1: Read the books. There is no substitute for reading authentic works of literature of diversity. Reflectively reading authentic works of literature of diversity can increase your cultural sensitivity to bias shown through use of language and stereotypical characterization or plot devices. By gaining heightened cultural sensitivity to issues of bias, you will be better able to select the literature best suited for a particular child or many children.

Tip #2: In addition to reading in order to know the books, it is important to know your students. Talk to them. Observe them. Record your observations in a journal. Reflect about what you notice and record. Meet your students' parents.

Tip #3: It is also helpful to know the reading interests/habits of your students. The survey form in Figure 7.1 can be administered to students at the beginning of the year to help you get to know more about them as readers. It can be administered to a whole class, in small groups, or individually, depending on the time available and the size of the class.

General Selection Questions

The following general questions are useful to ask with respect to the selection of literature of diversity for use in the classroom. These questions were asked during the title selection process for this book, and they are presented here under three categories: self-esteem, worldview, and themes.

Self-Esteem

1. Will the books I have chosen help my students see themselves in a positive way in literature and thereby affirm their self-worth?

Figure 7.1. Getting to Know You as a Reader

Name _____ **Age** _____

Directions: Check everything that shows who you are as a reader.

I like to read:

    before school _____   when I eat _____
    during school _____   before bed _____
    after school _____   all of the above _____
    none of the above ___   other times _____

I like to read:

    once a day _____   any time I can _____
    twice a day _____   not much _____

I like to read stories or books about _____

I want my stories to

    be funny _____   be beautiful _____
    have lots of action _____   make me think about something ___
    have easy words _____   have sad parts _____
    have words new to me _____   have scary parts _____
    have lots of characters talking _____

I prefer that stories or books be about real things.

Yes _____ No _____ Sometimes _____

I never buy books.   True _____ False _____

If someone were going to give me a book as a present (and money is not a problem for the giver), I would ask for _____

If I were going to buy a book for myself and money was not a problem, I would buy _____

One of my favorite stories is _____

I first came to know this story by

    hearing it read aloud to me by someone else _____
    reading it to myself _____

I think of myself as a person who

    loves to read _____   reads O.K., but only when I have to _____
    hates to read _____   likes to read sometimes _____

When I have free time, I like to

    read _____   play an instrument _____
    watch TV _____   play a sport _____
    listen to music _____   other _____

Someone still reads books or stories aloud to me. Yes ___ No ___

Do you have and read any of the following reading materials in your house?

    TV Guide _____   Magazines _____
    Newspaper(s) _____   Mail Order Catalogs or Advertisements ___

2. Will the books I have chosen which highlight a particular cultural/ethnic group help my students who identify with that group feel good about themselves as part of that cultural/ethnic group?

Worldview

1. Will the books I have chosen help my students expand their worldviews by increasing their knowledge, appreciation, and understanding of others different from themselves?

2. Will the books I have chosen facilitate my students seeing and discussing the differences and the similarities of people across cultures?

Themes

1. Will the books I have chosen help my students engage with themes such as friends, families, growing up, prejudice, racism, and war from multiple cultural experiences and perspectives?
2. Will the books I have chosen need guided discussion of the themes within them for my particular group of students? Am I prepared to facilitate those discussions?

Specific Method and Selection Criteria for This Book

Overall, a concerted effort was made to select works of quality literature that contribute to an understanding and appreciation of the diversity of human cultures and the breadth of human experience. As much as possible, works were selected that were written from an insider's perspective. When the work was written by an outsider, it was clearly written by an author who had made an effort through either research or immersion or both to know the culture of his/her characters or nonfiction topic.

The method of choosing these books was simple. I read and read. In preparing to write this book, I read hundreds of works of literature of diversity. Over the years, I have haunted bookstores and libraries, and have also ordered books from Trumpet, Troll, and Scholastic Book Clubs. I have shared this literature of diversity with the fourth-grade students I teach. I continue to seek new titles of literature of diversity to read. I continue to reread known works, and I continue to share these works with my students. The titles included in this book are the best of what I have read so far. They are works of power and grace.

Focus Questions Guiding Title Selection for This Book

Beyond the general selection questions, there were specific focus questions that remained uppermost in my mind as I read and reread potential works to include in the "Borders" chapters in this book. These questions were distilled from my understanding of the key selection issues of authenticity, bias, and balance that have been discussed here. The focus questions I asked as I read the books I considered for inclusion in this book are shown in Figure 7.2.

Figure 7.2. Focus Selection Questions

1. Does this book meet high standards of literary quality for its genre?
2. Is this book written from the perspective of a person from inside the culture represented in the book?
3. If the book is written by someone outside the culture represented in the book, has the author achieved authenticity through research and/or immersion in the culture?
4. Is there anything that would embarrass or offend me if this book was about me or my cultural group?
5. Does this book add to the balance of the total collection with respect to literary genres, cultural/ethnic groups, and themes?
6. Does this book reflect stereotypical characters and language?
7. In nonfiction, is there evidence of solid research?
8. Regardless of the genre, is the work rich in cultural details that enhance the quality and truth of the work?
9. Does this book engage me, capture my attention, make me want to keep reading?

Final Thoughts on Selection of Literature of Diversity

Through reading literature of diversity, we can increase our cultural awareness beyond the borders of our own culture, whatever that culture may be. We can look at the world from diverse perspectives and find our vision widened. As educators, this widening of vision aids us in the selection and use of literature of diversity. Bringing that literature into our classrooms can contribute to the development and actualization of an equitable literature curriculum, which may have far-reaching effects on our own lives, the lives of our students, and the future.

AFTERWORD

Teacher to Teacher

I once had a cup from which I drank innumerable cups of tea before and after school. It broke one day, but the saying written on it is forever imprinted in my mind: "A teacher touches a life and change begins . . ." I believe in teachers. I believe that teachers care about their world, and that they know within the core of their beings that they do have the ability to affect lives far beyond a given class or year. As a teacher, I believe that sometimes this knowledge makes us hold our heads high and sometimes it makes us quake. But, it is always there, under the surface of the daily chores of correcting papers, planning lessons, conferencing with parents and/or administrators, finding lost lunches, doing bulletin boards, healing children's hurt feelings, organizing the piles that come from everywhere, and on and on with all that makes up a teacher's working life. That core knowledge of our power to effect change is always there.

It seems to me that we are now poised on the brink of great changes in our world. Although it is not easy to be on such a cusp of change, it is challenging and exciting. Old paradigms are disintegrating and new ones are being born. There are great changes ahead. Those of us who work with children stand in a position of power and responsibility. We can help shape tomorrow through the choices we make today.

As I have persevered with writing this book, I have learned a great deal along the way, and I know I have more to learn with each passing day. Working with the books I've written about here has been enlightening, challenging, thought provoking, joyous, in short, everything. I wish I could sit down with everyone who will read this book, share a cup of tea, and talk endlessly about books, children we've known, our teaching lives, and living in our pluralistic world. I won't be able to do that. But, if each of you who read this book, and the books highlighted within it, will talk to someone else, then the power residing in this literature of diversity will spread.

I hope that we may learn to talk to each other in ways that will expand our understanding of one another and enhance our appreciation of our differences and our similarities whatever our ancestry, and thus one by one contribute to the healing of our world. I end as I began, sharing with you a poem. I wrote this poem while thinking about these books, the children and teachers who will read them, and our future.

How the Healing Began

Once upon a time
In those days between times
The people practiced the crossing of borders
By talking about and reading books
Which contained the histories, poems, and stories
Of all the people of the world
Told in their diverse voices.
And the people came to know more of themselves
And more of one another
And the knowing was good.
Through the awareness
Which came from their reading
And talking to one another
Compassion, respect, and understanding
Grew amongst them.
And thus began
The healing of the world
Once upon a time
In those days between times . . .

APPENDIX A

Thematic Groupings

Sample Thematic Units

Four possible themes using the books highlighted in Section II are suggested here: Families, Courage, Change, and Feelings. Someone else might come up with totally different themes, or even suggest different or additional books to be included in these four suggested themes. Such is the flexibility of this approach. The full bibliographic entry for the titles included in the themes here can be found in Section II. The publication dates given pertain to the paperback edition, unless HB denotes the hardback edition.

Theme 1. Families

Avi. (1996). *The Barn.*
Boyd, Candy Dawson. (1995). *Chevrolet Saturdays.*
Burgess, Barbara Hood. (1993). *Oren Bell.*
Cumpian, Carlos. (1994). *Latino Rainbow.*
Dorris, Michael. (1994). *Guests.*
Dorris, Michael. (1994). *Morning Girl.*
Fenner, Carol. (1996). *Yolanda's Genius.*
Fox, Paula. (1993). *Monkey Island.*
George, Jean Craighead. (1996). *Julie.*
Greenfield, Eloise. (1988). *Nathaniel Talking.*
Houston, James. (1994). *Drifting Snow: An Arctic Search.*
Joseph, Lynn. (1992). *Coconut Kind of Day, Island Poems.*
Katz, William Loren. (1993). *A History of Multicultural America: Minorities Today.*
Mathis, Sharon Bell. (1986). *The Hundred Penny Box.*
Medearis, Angela Shelf. (1991). *Dancing With the Indians.* (HB).

Myers, Walter Dean. (1995). *Glorious Angels: A Celebration of Children.*
Myers, Walter Dean. (1991). *Me, Mop, and the Moondance Kid.*
Namioka, Lensey. (1994). *Yang the Youngest and His Terrible Ear.*
Namioka, Lensey. (1996). *Yang the Third and Her Impossible Family.*
Soto, Gary. (1991). *Baseball in April and Other Stories.*
Soto, Gary. (1994). *Neighborhood Odes.*
Soto, Gary. (1995). *The Pool Party.*
Strickland, Dorothy S. & Strickland, Michael R. (1996). *Families: Poems Celebrating the African American Experience.*
Uchida, Yoshiko. (1993). *The Best Bad Thing.*
Uchida, Yoshiko. (1987). *The Invisible Thread.* (HB).
Uchida, Yoshiko. (1989). *Journey Home.*
Yep, Laurence. (1990). *Child of the Owl.*
Yep, Laurence. (1996). *The Lost Garden.*
Yep, Laurence. (1992). *The Star Fisher.*

Theme 2. Courage

Ackerman, Karen. (1994). *The Night Crossing.*
Adler, David A. (1990). *We Remember the Holocaust.*
Altman, Susan and Lechner, Susan. (1993). *Followers of the North Star. Rhymes About African American Heroes, Heroines, and Historical Times.*
Baillie, Allan. (1994). *Little Brother.*
Brown, Dee. (1994). *Wounded Knee: An Indian History of the American West.*
Conlon-McKenna, Marita. (1992). *Under the Hawthorn Tree.*
Cox, Clinton. (1991). *Undying Glory: The True Story of the Massachusetts 54th Regiment.*
De Trevino, Elizabeth Borton. (1996). *El Guero: A True Adventure Story.*
Dorris, Michael. (1997). *Sees Behind Trees.*
Drucker, Malka and Halperin, Michael. (1994). *Jacob's Rescue: A Holocaust Story.*
Ferris, Jeri. (1991). *Native American Doctor: The Story of Susan Laflesche Picotte.*
Filipovic, Zlata. (1994). *Zlata's Diary.*
Hamilton, Virginia. (1989). *Willie Bea and the Time the Martians Landed.*
Hill, Kirkpatrick. (1992). *Toughboy and Sister.*
Ho, Minfong. (1993). *The Clay Marble.*
...*I Never Saw Another Butterfly...Children's Drawings and Poems From Terezin Concentration Camp 1942–1944.* (1978).
Lester, Julius. (1968). *To Be a Slave.*
Lowry, Lois. (1990). *Number the Stars.*
McKissack, Patricia and McKissack, Fredrick. (1992). *Sojourner truth: Ain't I a Woman?*
Naidoo, Beverly. (1986). *Journey to Jo'Burg: A South African Story.*
Price, Joan. (1982). *Truth Is a Bright Star.*
Salisbury, Graham. (1995). *Under the Blood-Red Sun.*
Soto, Gary. (1996). *Boys at Work.*
Taylor, Mildred D. (1989). *The Friendship and the Gold Cadillac.*
Turcotte, Mark. (1995). *Songs of Our Ancestors. Poems About Native Americans.*
Watkins, Yoko Kawashima. (1994). *So Far From the Bamboo Grove.*
Yep, Laurence. (1975). *Dragonwings.*

Yep, Laurence. (1995). *Dragon's Gate.*

Theme 3. Change

Armstrong, Jennifer. (1993). *Steal Away . . . to Freedom.*
Berry, James. (1994). *Ajeemah and His Son.*
Bruchac, Joseph and London, Jonathan. (1995). *Thirteen Moons on Turtle's Back: A Native American Year of Moons.*
Choi, Sook Nyui. (1993). *Year of Impossible Goodbyes.*
Conlon-McKenna, Marita. (1994). *Wildflower Girl.*
Fleischman, Paul. (1995). *Bull Run.*
Freedman, Russell. (1992). *Immigrant Kids.*
George, Jean Craighead. (1972). *Julie of the Wolves.*
Hamilton, Virginia. (1991). *In the Beginning: Creation Stories From Around the World.*
Hansen, Joyce. (1994). *The Captive.*
Hesse, Karen. (1993). *Letters From Rifka.*
Hilts, Len. (1987). *Quanah Parker.*
Houston, Jeanne Wakatsuki and Houston, James D. (1974). *Farewell to Manzanar.*
Johnson, James Weldon. (1994). *Lift Every Voice and Sing.*
Johnston, Norma. (1995). *Remember the Ladies: The First Women's Rights Convention.*
Kroeber, Theodora. (1989). *Ishi, Last of His Tribe.*
Lai, Him Mark, Lim, Genny, and Yung, Judy. (1996). *Island: Poetry and History of Chinese Immigrants on Angel Island 1910–1940.*
Lord, Bette Bao. (1987). *In the Year of the Boar and Jackie Robinson.*
McKissack, Patricia and McKissack, Fredrick, Jr. (1994). *Black Diamond: The Story of the Negro Baseball Leagues.*
McKissack, Patricia and McKissack, Fredrick L. (1996). *Rebels Against Slavery: American Slave Revolts.*
Mead, Alice. (1997). *Junebug.*
Myers, Walter Dean. (1991). *Now Is Your Time! The African-American Struggle for Freedom.*
Parks, Rosa with Jim Haskins. (1994). *Rosa Parks: My Story.*
Porter, Connie. (1994). *Meet Addy, an American Girl. Book One.*
Smucker, Barbara. (1979). *Runaway to Freedom: A Story of the Underground Railway.*
Soto, Gary. (1995). *The Pool Party.*
Soto, Gary. (1991). *Taking Sides.*
Stanley, Jerry. (1992). *Children of the Dust Bowl: The True Story of the School at Weedpatch Camp.*
Whelan, Gloria. (1993). *Goodbye, Vietnam.*
Whelan, Gloria. (1996). *Night of the Full Moon.*
Yarbrough, Camille. (1990). *The Shimmershine Queens.*

Theme 4. Feelings

Adoff, Arnold. (1992). *All the Colors of the Race.*

Bealer, Alex W. (1996). *Only the Names Remain: The Cherokees and the Trail of Tears.*
Carlson, Lori M. and Ventura, Cynthia L. (Eds.). (1990). *Where Angels Glide at Dawn: New Stories From Latin America.*
Coerr, Eleanor. (1994). *Mieko and the Fifth Treasure.*
Coerr, Eleanor. (1979). *Sadako and the Thousand Paper Cranes.*
Cumpian, Carlos. (1994). *Latino Rainbow.*
George, Chief Dan. (1994). *My Heart Soars.*
Greenfield, Eloise. (1992). *Honey, I Love and Other Love Poems.*
Hamilton, Virginia. (1991). *Cousins.*
Hautzig, Esther. (1968). *The Endless Steppe. Growing up in Siberia.* (HB).
Hirschfelder, Arlene and Singer, Beverly R. (1992). *Rising Voices: Writings of Young Native Americans.*
Hughes, Langston. (1996). *The Dream Keeper and Other Poems.*
Izuki, Steven. (1994). *Believers in America: Poems About Americans of Asian and Pacific Islander Descent.*
Levine, Ellen. (1994). *Freedom's Children: Young Civil Rights Activists Tell Their Own Stories.*
McLain, Gary. (1990). *The Indian Way: Learning to Communicate With Mother Earth.*
Mohr, Nicholasa. (1990). *Felita.*
Mohr, Nicholasa. (1989). *Going Home.*
Nye, Naomi Shihab (Ed.). (1992). *This Same Sky: A Collection of Poems From Around the World.*
Pettit, Jayne. (1993). *A Place to Hide: True Stories of Holocaust Rescues.*
Soto, Gary. (1991). *Baseball in April and Other Stories.*
Spinelli, Jerry. (1991). *Maniac Magee.*
Taylor, Mildred D. (1992). *Mississippi Bridge.*
Taylor, Mildred D. (1991). *Roll of Thunder, Hear My Cry.*
Taylor, Mildred D. (1979). *Song of the Trees.*
Uchida, Yoshiko. (1993). *A Jar of Dreams.*
Yep, Laurence. (1997). *Thief of Hearts.*

Appendix B

Cultural/Ethnic Groupings

The titles in this appendix are grouped according to the focus of the work: (1) single cultural/ethnic perspective of groups within the United States, (2) multiethnic perspective within the U.S., and (3) global perspective beyond the borders of the U.S. The full bibliographic entries for the titles in this appendix can be found in Section II, Chapters 3, 4, and 5. The publication dates given here pertain to the paperback edition, unless HB denotes the hardback edition.

Within the United States

African American

Altman, Susan and Lechner, Susan. (1993). *Followers of the North Star: Rhymes About African American Heroes, Heroines, and Historical Times.*
Boyd, Candy Dawson. (1995). *Chevrolet Saturdays.*
Burgess, Barbara Hood. (1993). *Oren Bell.*
Cox, Clinton. (1991). *Undying Glory: The Story of the Massachusetts 54th Regiment.*
Fenner, Carol. (1996). *Yolanda's Genius.*
Greenfield, Eloise. (1992). *Honey, I Love and Other Love Poems.*
Greenfield, Eloise. (1988). *Nathaniel Talking.*
Hamilton, Virginia. (1991). *Cousins.*
Hamilton, Virginia. (1993). *The House of Dies Drear.*
Hamilton, Virginia. (1988). *The Mystery of Drear House.*
Hamilton, Virginia. (1994). *The People Could Fly: American Black Folktales.*
Hamilton, Virginia. (1989). *Willie Bea and the Time the Martians Landed.*
Hansen, Joyce. (1994). *The Captive.*
Hughes, Langston. (1996). *The Dream Keeper and Other Poems.*
Johnson, James Weldon. (1994). *Lift Every Voice and Sing.*

Lester, Julius. (1968). *To Be a Slave*. (HB).
Levine, Ellen. (1994). *Freedom's Children. Young Civil Rights Activists Tell Their Own Stories.*
Mathis, Sharon Bell. (1986). *The Hundred Penny Box.*
McKissack, Patricia C. (1993). *The Dark-Thirty: Southern Tales of the Supernatural.*
McKissack, Patricia C. and McKissack, Fredrick L. (1996). *Rebels Against Slavery: American Slave Revolts.*
McKissack, Patricia and McKissack, Frederick, Jr. (1994). *Black Diamond: The Story of the Negro Baseball Leagues.*
McKissack, Patricia and McKissack, Fredrick. (1992). *Sojourner Truth: Ain't I a Woman?*
Mead, Alice. (1997). *Junebug.*
Myers, Walter Dean. (1991). *Now Is Your Time! The African-American Struggle for Freedom.*
Parks, Rosa with Haskins, Jim. (1994). *Rosa Parks: My Story.*
Pelz, Ruth. (1990). *Black Heroes of the Wild West.*
Porter, Connie. (1994). *Addy Learns a Lesson.*
Porter, Connie. (1994). *Meet Addy, an American Girl: Book One.*
Porter, Connie. (1994). *Addy's Surprise.*
Smucker, Barbara. (1979). *Runaway to Freedom: A Story of the Underground Railway.*
Strickland, Dorothy S. and Strickland, Michael R. (Eds.). (1996). *Families: Poems Celebrating the African American Experience.*
Strickland, Dorothy S. (Ed.). (1986). *Listen Children: An Anthology of Black Literature.*
Taylor, Mildred D. (1989). *The Friendship and the Gold Cadillac.*
Taylor, Mildred D. (1991). *Roll of Thunder, Hear My Cry.*
Taylor, Mildred D. (1979). *Song of the Trees.*
Thomas, Joyce Carol. (1993). *Brown Honey in Broomwheat Tea.*
Yarbrough, Camille. (1990). *The Shimmershine Queens.*
Yates, Elizabeth. (1950). *Amos Fortune Free Man.*

Asian American

Houston, Jeanne Wakatsuki and Houston, James D. (1974). *Farewell to Manzanar.*
Izuki, Steven. (1994). *Believers in America: Poems About Americans of Asian and Pacific Islander Descent.*
Lai, Him Mark, Lim, Genny, and Yung, Judy. (1996). *Island: Poetry and History of Chinese Immigrants on Angel Island, 1910–1940.*
Lord, Bette Bao. (1987). *In the Year of the Boar and Jackie Robinson.*
Uchida, Yoshiko. (1993). *The Best Bad Thing.*
Uchida, Yoshiko. (1987). *The Invisible Thread.*
Uchida, Yoshiko. (1993). *A Jar of Dreams.*
Uchida, Yoshiko. (1989). *Journey Home.*
Yep, Laurence. (1990). *Child of the Owl.*
Yep, Laurence. (1975). *Dragonwings.*
Yep, Laurence. (1995). *Dragon's Gate.*
Yep, Laurence. (1996). *The Lost Garden.*

Yep, Laurence. (1992). *The Rainbow People*.
Yep, Laurence. (1992). *The Star Fisher*.
Yep, Laurence. (1997). *Thief of Hearts*.

Euro-American

Avi. *The Barn*. (1994). (HB).
Freedman, Russell. (1980). *Immigrant Kids*. (HB). 1992. (PB).
Johnston, Norma. (1995). *Remember the Ladies: The First Women's Rights Convention*.
Stanley, Jerry. (1992). *Children of the Dust Bowl: The True Story of the School at Weedpatch Camp*.

Hispanic American

Cumpian, Carlos. (1994). *Latino Rainbow*.
Mohr, Nicholasa. (1990). *Felita*.
Mohr, Nicholasa. (1989). *Going Home*.
Palacios, Argentina. (1994). *Standing Tall: The Stories of Ten Hispanic Americans*.
Soto, Gary. (1991). *Baseball in April and Other Stories*.
Soto, Gary. (1996). *Boys at Work*.
Soto, Gary. (1994). *Neighborhood Odes*.
Soto, Gary. (1995). *The Pool Party*.
Soto, Gary. (1991). *Taking Sides*.

Native American

Baylor, Byrd. (1997). *The Way to Make Perfect Mountains: Native American Legends of Sacred Mountains*.
Bealer, Alex W. (1996). *Only the Names Remain. The Cherokees and the Trail of Tears*.
Brown, Dee. (1974). *Wounded Knee: An Indian History of the American West*.
Bruchac, Joseph. (1990). *Return of the Sun: Native American Tales from the Northeast Woodlands*.
Bruchac, Joseph and London, Jonathan. (1995). *Thirteen Moons on Turtle's Back: A Native American Year of Moons*.
Dorris, Michael. (1994). *Guests*.
Dorris, Michael. (1994). *Morning Girl*.
Dorris, Michael. (1997). *Sees Behind Trees*.
Ferris, Jeri. (1991). *Native American Doctor: The Story of Susan Laflesche Picotte*.
Freedman, Russell. (1991). *Indian Chiefs*.
Freedman, Russell. (1997). *The Life and Death of Crazy Horse*.
George, Chief Dan. (1994). *My Heart Soars*.
George, Jean Craighead. (1972). *Julie of the Wolves*.
George, Jean Craighead. (1996). *Julie*.
Hill, Kirkpatrick. (1992). *Toughboy and Sister*.
Hill, Kirkpatrick. (1995). *Winter Camp*.
Hilts, Len. (1987). *Quanah Parker*.
Hirschfelder, Arlene and Singer, Beverly R. (1992). *Rising voices: Writings of Young Native Americans*.

Houston, James. (1994). *Drifting Snow: An Arctic Search Novel.*
Kroeber, Theodora. (1989). *Ishi, Last of His Tribe.*
McLain, Gary. (1990). *The Indian Way: Learning to Communicate With Mother Earth.*
Price, Joan. (1982). *Truth Is a Bright Star.*
Sneve, Virginia Driving Hawk. (Ed.). (1989). *Dancing Teepees: Poems of American Indian Youth.*
Thomasma, Kenneth. (1993). *Kunu: Escape on the Missouri.*
Turcotte, Mark. (1995). *Songs of Our Ancestors. Poems About Native Americans.*

Multiethnic

These titles highlight main characters and/or perspectives of more than one cultural/ethnic group within the United States.

Adoff, Arnold. (1992). *All the Colors of the Race.*
Armstrong, Jennifer. (1993). *Steal Away . . . to Freedom.*
Fleischman, Paul. (1995). *Bull Run.*
Fox, Paula. (1993). *Monkey Island.*
Katz, William Loren. (1993). *A History of Multicultural America: Minorities Today.*
Keehn, Sally M. (1997). *Moon of Two Dark Horses.*
Medearis, Angela Shelf. (1991). *Dancing With the Indians.*
Myers, Walter Dean. (1991). *Me, Mop, and the Moondance Kid.*
Myers, Walter Dean. (1994). *Mop, Moondance and the Nagasaki Knights.*
Namioka, Lensey. (1996). *Yang the Third and Her Impossible Family.*
Namioka, Lensey. (1994). *Yang the Youngest and His Terrible Ear.*
Salisbury, Graham. (1995). *Under the Blood-Red Sun.*
Spinelli, Jerry. (1991). *Maniac Magee.*
Taylor, Mildred D. (1992). *Mississippi Bridge.*
Whelan, Gloria. (1996). *Night of the Full Moon.*

Beyond the Borders of the United States

These titles are focused on a cultural/ethnic group outside the United States.

Ackerman, Karen. (1994). *The Night Crossing.*
Adler, David A. (1990). *We Remember the Holocaust.*
Baillie, Allan. (1994). *Little Brother.*
Berry, James. (1994). *Ajeemah and His Son.*
Carlson, Lori M. and Ventura, Cynthia. (Ed.). (1990). *Where Angels Glide at Dawn: New Stories From Latin America.*
Choi, Sook Nyui. (1995). *Echoes of the White Giraffe.*
Choi, Sook Nyui. (1993). *Year of Impossible Goodbyes.*
Coerr, Eleanor. (1994). *Mieko and the Fifth Treasure.*
Coerr, Eleanor. (1979). *Sadako and the Thousand Paper Cranes.*
Conlon-McKenna, Marita. (1992). *Under the Hawthorn Tree.*

Conlon-McKenna, Marita. (1994). *Wildflower Girl*.
De Trevino, Elizabeth Borton. (1996). *El Guero: A True Adventure Story*.
Drucker, Malka and Halperin, Michael. (1994). *Jacob's Rescue: A Holocaust Story*.
Filipovic, Zlata. (1994). *Zlata's Diary*.
Hautzig, Esther. (1968). *The Endless Steppe. Growing Up in Siberia*. (HB).
Hesse, Karen. (1993). *Letters From Rifka*.
Ho, Minfong. (1993). *The Clay Marble*.
... *I Never Saw Another Butterfly ... Children's Drawings and Poems From Terezin Concentration Camp 1942–1944*. (1978).
Joseph, Lynn. (1992). *Coconut Kind of Day, Island Poems*.
Levitin, Sonia. (1987). *Journey to America*.
Lowry, Lois. (1990). *Number the Stars*.
Naidoo, Beverly. (1986). *Journey to Jo'burg: A South African Story*.
Pettit, Jayne. (1993). *A Place to Hide. True Stories of Holocaust Rescues*.
Watkins, Yoko Kawashima. (1994). *So Far From the Bamboo Grove*.
Whelan, Gloria. (1993). *Goodbye, Vietnam*.

Global

These titles include works (i.e., folktales, poetry) that reflect multiple cultural/ethnic groups around the globe.

Baylor, Byrd. (1986). *The Way to Start a Day*.
Cole, Joanna. (Ed.). (1982). *Best-Loved Folktales of the World*.
Hamilton, Virginia. (1991). *In the Beginning. Creation Stories from Around the World*.
Myers, Walter Dean. (1995). *Glorious Angels: A Celebration of Children*.
Nye, Naomi Shihab. (Ed.). (1992). *This Same Sky: A Collection of Poems From Around the World*.
Phelps, Ethel Johnston. (Ed.). (1982). *The Maid of the North: Feminist Folk Tales From Around the World*.
Yolen, Jane. (Ed.). (1986). *Favorite Folktales From Around the World*.

APPENDIX C

Literary Genre Groupings

In this appendix, the titles have been grouped by genres to help with curriculum planning. The full bibliographic entries can be found in Chapters 3, 4, and 5. The publication dates given here pertain to the paperback date edition, unless HB denotes the hardback edition.

Biography and Autobiography

Drucker, Malka and Halperin, Michael. (1994). *Jacob's Rescue: A Holocaust Story*.
Ferris, Jeri. (1991). *Native American Doctor: The Story of Susan Laflesche Picotte*.
Filipovic, Zlata. (1994). *Zlata's Diary*.
Freedman, Russell. (1991). *Indian Chiefs*.
Freedman, Russell. (1997). *The Life and Death of Crazy Horse*.
Hautzig, Esther. (1968). *The Endless Steppe. Growing Up in Siberia*. (HB).
Hilts, Len. (1987). *Quanah Parker*.
Houston, Jeanne Wakatsuki and Houston, James D. (1974). *Farewell to Manzanar*.
Kroeber, Theodora. (1989). *Ishi, Last of His Tribe*.
McKissack, Patricia and McKissack, Fredrick. (1992). *Sojourner Truth: Ain't I a Woman?*
Palacios, Argentina. (1994). *Standing tall: The Stories of Ten Hispanic Americans*.
Parks, Rosa with Haskins, Jim. (1994). *Rosa Parks: My Story*.
Pelz, Ruth. (1990). *Black Heroes of the Wild West*.
Pettit, Jayne. (1993). *A Place to Hide: True Stories of Holocaust Rescues*.
Uchida, Yoshiko. (1987). *The Invisible Thread*.
Watkins, Yoko Kawashima. (1994). *So Far From the Bamboo Grove*.
Yates, Elizabeth. (1950). *Amos Fortune Free Man*.
Yep, Laurence. (1996). *The Lost Garden*.

Contemporary Realistic Fiction

Baillie, Allan. (1994). *Little Brother*.
Boyd, Candy Dawson. (1995). *Chevrolet Saturdays*.
Burgess, Barbara Hood. (1993). *Oren Bell*.

Choi, Sook Nyui. (1995). *Echoes of the White Giraffe*.
Choi, Sook Nyui. (1993). *Year of Impossible Goodbyes*.
Fenner, Carol. (1996). *Yolanda's Genius*.
Fox, Paula. (1993). *Monkey Island*.
George, Jean Craighead. (1972). *Julie of the Wolves*.
George, Jean Craighead. (1996). *Julie*.
Hamilton, Virginia. (1991). *Cousins*.
Hamilton, Virginia. (1993). *The House of Dies Drear*.
Hill, Kirkpatrick. (1992). *Toughboy and Sister*.
Hill, Kirkpatrick. (1995). *Winter Camp*.
Ho, Minfong. (1993). *The Clay Marble*.
Houston, James. (1994). *Drifting Snow: An Arctic Novel*.
Mathis, Sharon Bell. (1986). *The Hundred Penny Box*.
Mead, Alice. (1997). *Junebug*.
Mohr, Nicholasa. (1990). *Felita*.
Mohr, Nicholasa. (1989). *Going Home*.
Myers, Walter Dean. (1991). *Me, Mop, and the Moondance Kid*.
Myers, Walter Dean. (1994). *Mop, Moondance and the Nagasaki Knights*.
Naidoo, Beverly. (1986). *Journey to Jo'burg: A South African Story*.
Namioka, Lensey. (1996). *Yang the Third and Her Impossible Family*.
Namioka, Lensey. (1994). *Yang the Youngest and His Terrible Ear*.
Soto, Gary. (1996). *Boys at Work*.
Soto, Gary. (1995). *The Pool Party*.
Soto, Gary. (1991). *Taking Sides*.
Spinelli, Jerry. (1991). *Maniac Magee*.
Whelan, Gloria. (1993). *Goodbye, Vietnam*.
Yarbrough, Camille. (1990). *The Shimmershine Queens*.
Yep, Laurence. (1990). *Child of the Owl*.
Yep, Laurence. (1997). *Thief of Hearts*.

Folklore Anthologies

Bruchac, Joseph. (1990). *Return of the Sun: Native American Tales From the Northeast Woodlands*.
Cole, Joanna (Ed.). (1982). *Best-Loved Folktales of the World*.
Hamilton, Virginia. (1991). *In the Beginning. Creation Stories From Around the World*.
Hamilton, Virginia. (1994). *The People Could Fly: American Black Folktales*.
McKissack, Patricia C. (1993). *The Dark-Thirty: Southern Tales of the Supernatural*.
McLain, Gary. (1990). *The Indian Way: Learning to Communicate With Mother Earth*.
Phelps, Ethel Johnston. (1982). *The Maid of the North: Feminist Folk Tales From Around the World*.
Yep, Laurence. (1992). *The Rainbow People*.
Yolen, Jane. (Ed.). (1986). *Favorite Folktales From Around the World*.

History

Adler, David A. (1990). *We Remember the Holocaust*.
Bealer, Alex W. (1996). *Only the Names Remain. The Cherokees and the Trail of Tears*.
Brown, Dee. (1994). *Wounded Knee: An Indian History of the American West*.
Cox, Clinton. (1991). *Undying Glory: The Story of the Massachusetts 54th Regiment*.

Freedman, Russell. (1992). *Immigrant Kids*.
Johnston, Norma. (1995). *Remember the Ladies: The First Women's Rights Convention*.
Katz, William Loren. (1993). *A History of Multicultural America: Minorities Today*.
Lai, Him Mark, Lim, Genny, & Yung, Judy. (1996). *Island: Poetry and History of Chinese Immigrants on Angel Island, 1910–1940*.
Lester, Julius. (1968). *To Be a Slave*. (HB).
Levine, Ellen. (1994). *Freedom's Children: Young Civil Rights Activists Tell Their Own Stories*.
McKissack, Patricia and McKissack, Frederick, Jr. (1994). *Black Diamond: The Story of the Negro Baseball Leagues*.
McKissack, Patricia C. and Mckissack, Fredrick L. (1996). *Rebels Against Slavery. American Slave Revolts*.
Myers, Walter Dean. (1991). *Now is Your Time! The African-American Struggle for Freedom*.
Stanley, Jerry. (1992). *Children of the Dust Bowl: The True Story of the School at Weedpatch Camp*.

Historical Fiction

Ackerman, Karen. (1994). *The Night Crossing*.
Armstrong, Jennifer. (1993). *Steal Away . . . to Freedom*.
Avi. (1996). *The Barn*.
Berry, James. (1994). *Ajeemah and His Son*.
Coerr, Eleanor. (1994). *Mieko and the Fifth Treasure*.
Coerr, Eleanor. (1979). *Sadako and the Thousand Paper Cranes*.
Conlon-McKenna, Marita. (1992). *Under the Hawthorn*.
Conlon-McKenna, Marita. (1994). *Wildflower Girl*.
De Trevino, Elizabeth Borton. (1996). *El Guero: A True Adventure Story*.
Dorris, Michael. (1994). *Guests*.
Dorris, Michael. (1994). *Morning Girl*.
Dorris, Michael. (1997). *Sees Behind Trees*.
Fleischman, Paul. (1995). *Bull Run*.
Hamilton, Virginia. (1989). *Willie Bea and the Time the Martians Landed*.
Hansen, Joyce. (1994). *The Captive*.
Hesse, Karen. (1993). *Letters From Rifka*.
Keehn, Sally M. (1997). *Moon of Two Dark Horses*.
Levitin, Sonia. (1987). *Journey to America*.
Lord, Bette Bao. (1987). *In the Year of the Boar and Jackie Robinson*.
Lowry, Lois. (1990). *Number the Stars*.
Porter, Connie. (1994). *Addy Learns a Lesson*.
Porter, Connie. (1994). *Meet Addy, an American Girl. Book One*.
Porter, Connie. (1994). *Addy's Surprise*.
Price, Joan. (1982). *Truth is a Bright Star*.
Salisbury, Graham. (1995). *Under the Blood-Red Sun*.
Smucker, Barbara. (1979). *Runaway to Freedom: A Story of the Underground Railway*.
Taylor, Mildred D. (1989). *The Friendship and the Gold Cadillac*.
Taylor, Mildred D. (1992). *Mississippi Bridge*.
Taylor, Mildred D. (1991). *Roll of Thunder, Hear My Cry*.
Taylor, Mildred D. (1979). *Song of the Trees*.

Thomasma, Kenneth. (1993). *Kunu: Escape on the Missouri.*
Uchida, Yoshiko. (1993). *A Jar of Dreams.*
Uchida, Yoshiko. (1993). *The Best Bad Thing.*
Uchida, Yoshiko. (1989). *Journey Home.*
Whelan, Gloria. (1996). *Night of the Full Moon.*
Yep, Laurence. (1975). *Dragonwings.*
Yep, Laurence. (1995). *Dragon's Gate.*
Yep, Laurence. (1992). *The Star Fisher.*

Poetry

Adoff, Arnold. (1992). *All the Colors of the Race.*
Altman, Susan and Lechner, Susan. (1993). *Followers of the North Star. Rhymes About African American Heroes, Heroines, and Historical Times.*
Baylor, Byrd. (1997). *The Way to Make Perfect Mountains: Native American Legends of Sacred Mountains.*
Baylor, Byrd. (1986). *The Way to Start a Day.*
Bruchac, Joseph and London, Jonathan. (1995). *Thirteen Moons on Turtle's Back: A Native American Year of Moons.*
Cumpian, Carlos. (1994). *Latino Rainbow.*
George, Chief Dan. (1994). *My Heart Soars.*
Greenfield, Eloise. (1986). *Honey, I Love and Other Love Poems.*
Greenfield, Eloise. (1988). *Nathaniel Talking.*
Hirschfelder, Arlene and Singer, Beverly R. (1992). *Rising Voices: Writings of Young Native Americans.*
Hughes, Langston. (1996). *The Dream Keeper and Other Poems.*
... I Never Saw Another Butterfly ... Children's Drawings and Poems From Terezin Concentration Camp 1942-1944. (1978).
Izuki, Steven. (1994). *Believers in America: Poems About Americans of Asian and Pacific Islander Descent.*
Johnson, James Weldon. (1994). *Lift Every Voice and Sing.*
Joseph, Lynn. (1992). *Coconut Kind of Day, Island Poems.*
Medearis, Angela Shelf. (1991). *Dancing With the Indians.*
Myers, Walter Dean. (1995). *Glorious Angels: A Celebration of Children.*
Nye, Naomi Shihab. (Ed.). (1992). *This Same Sky: A Collection of Poems From Around the World.*
Sneve, Virginia Driving Hawk. (Ed.). (1989). *Dancing Teepees: Poems of American Indian Youth.*
Soto, Gary. (1994). *Neighborhood Odes.*
Strickland, Dorothy S. and Strickland, Michael R. (Eds.). (1996). *Families: Poems Celebrating the African American Experience.*
Thomas, Joyce Carol. (1993). *Brown Honey in Broomwheat Tea.*
Turcotte, Mark. (1995). *Songs of Our Ancestors: Poems About Native Americans.*

Short Stories and Sometimes a Bit More

Carlson, Lori M. and Ventura, Cynthia L. (Eds.). (1990). *Where Angels Glide at Dawn: New stories from Latin America.*
Soto, Gary. (1991). *Baseball in April and Other Stories.*
Strickland, Dorothy S. (Ed.). (1986). *Listen Children: An Anthology of Black Literature.*

References

Anaya, R. (1992). The censorship of neglect. *English Journal, 81* (5), 18–20.

Applebee, A. N. (1992). Stability and change in the high-school canon. *English Journal, 81* (5), 27–32.

Bishop, R. S. (1987). Extending multicultural understanding through children's books. In B. E. Cullinan (Ed.), *Children's literature in the reading program* (pp. 60–67). Newark, DE: International Reading Association.

Bishop, R. S. (1992). Multicultural literature for children: Making informed choices. In V. J. Harris (Ed.), *Teaching multicultural literature in grades K–8* (pp. 37–53). Norwood, MA: Christopher-Gordon Publishers.

Bishop, R. S. (Ed.). (1994). *Kaleidoscope, A multicultural booklist for grades K–8.* Urbana, IL: National Council of Teachers of English.

Cai, M., & Bishop, R. S. (1994). Multicultural literature for children: Towards a clarification of the concept. In A. H. Dyson & C. Genishi (Eds.). *The need for story—Cultural diversity in classroom and community* (pp. 57–71). Urbana, IL: National Council of Teachers of English.

Daniels, H. (1994). *Literature circles: Voice and choice in the student-centered classroom.* York, ME: Stenhouse Publishers.

Day, F. A. (1994). Evaluating children's books for bias. In F. A. Day, *Multicultural voices in contemporary literature: A resource for teachers* (pp. 5–8). Portsmouth, NH: Heinemann.

De La Luz Reyes, M., Laliberty, E. A., & Orbanosky, J. M. (1993). Emerging biliteracy and cross-cultural sensitivity in a language arts classroom. *Language Arts, 70,* 659–668.

Fleischman, P. (1989). *Joyful noise: Poems for two voices.* Illustrated by E. Beddows. New York: The Trumpet Club.

Ford, M. T. (1994, July 18). The cult of multiculturalism. *Publishers Weekly,* pp. 30–33.

Freire, P. (1983, October). The importance of the act of reading. *Education Digest,* pp. 11–13.

Goldenhersh, B. L. (1992). *Read it with bookmarks.* Belleville, IL: Classroom Catalyst Press.

Hancock, J., & Hill, S. (Eds.). (1988). *Literature-based reading programs at work.* Portsmouth, NH: Heinemann Educational Books.

Harris, V. J. (1994). Multiculturalism and children's literature. In F. Lehr & J. Osborn (Eds.), *Reading, language, and literacy: Instruction for the twenty-first century* (pp. 201–214). Hillsdale, NJ: Lawrence Erlbaum.

Henderson, V. M. (1991). The development of self-esteem in children of color. In M. V. Lindgren (Ed.), *The multicolored mirror: Cultural substance in literature for children and young adults* (pp. 15–30). Fort Atkinson, WI: Highsmith Press.

Hickman, J., & Cullinan, B. (Eds.). (1989). *Children's literature in the classroom: Weaving Charlotte's web.* Norwood, MA: Christopher-Gordon Publishers.

Hickman, J., Cullinan, B. E., & Hepler, S. (Eds.). (1994). *Children's Literature in the classroom: Extending Charlotte's web.* Norwood, MA: Christopher-Gordon Publishers.

Hill, B. C., Johnson, N. J., & Noe, K. L. S. (1995). *Literature circles and response.* Norwood, MA: Christopher-Gordon Publishers.

Horning, K. T., & Kruse, G. M. (1991). Looking into the mirror: Considerations behind the reflections. In M. V. Lindgren (Ed.), *The multicolored mirror: Cultural substance in literature for children and young adults* (pp. 1–13). Fort Atkinson, WI: Highsmith Press.

Howard, E. F. (1991). Authentic multicultural literature for children: An author's perspective. In M. V. Lindgren (Ed.), *The multicolored mirror: Cultural substance in literature for children and young adults* (pp. 91–99). Fort Atkinson, WI: Highsmith Press.

Jay, G. S. (1991). The end of "American" literature: Toward a multicultural practice. *College English, 53,* 264–281.

Johnson, L., & Smith, S. (1993). *Dealing with diversity through multicultural fiction: Library-classroom partnerships.* Chicago and London: American Library Association.

Johnson, T. D., & Louis, D. R. (1987). *Literacy through literature.* Portsmouth, NH: Heinemann Educational Books.

Kruse, G. M. (1992). No single season: Multicultural literature for all children. *Wilson Library Bulletin, 66* (6), 30–33, 122.

Larrick, N. (1965, September 11). The all-white world of children's books. *Saturday Review,* pp. 63–65, 84–85.

Moss, J. F. (1984). *Focus units in literature: A handbook for elementary school teachers.* Urbana, IL: National Council of Teachers of English.

Nieto, S. (1992). We have stories to tell: A case study of Puerto Ricans in children's books. In V. J. Harris (Ed.), *Teaching multicultural literature in grades K–8* (pp. 171–201). Norwood, MA: Christopher-Gordon Publishers.

Norton, D. E. (1990). Teaching multicultural literature in the reading curriculum. *The Reading Teacher, 44,* 28–40.

Nye, N. S. (1995). *The tree is older than you are: A bilingual gathering of poems & stories from Mexico with paintings by Mexican artists.* New York: Simon & Schuster.

Powell, R. E. (1992). Goals for the language arts program: Toward a democratic vision. *Language Arts, 69,* 342–349.

Reimer, K. M. (1992). Multiethnic literature: Holding fast to dreams. *Language Arts, 69,* pp. 14–21.

Robb, L. (1994). *Whole language, whole learners: Creating a literature-centered classroom.* New York: Quill.

Roser, N. L., & Martinez, M. G. (Eds.). (1995). *Book talk and beyond: Children and teachers respond to literature.* Newark, DE: International Reading Association.

Rothlein, L., & Meinbach, A. M. (1991). *The literature connection: Using children's books in the classroom.* Glenview, IL: Scott, Foresman and Company.

Rudman, M. K. (Ed.). (1989). Children's literature: Resource for the classroom. Norwood, MA: Christopher-Gordon Publishers.

Short, K. G., & Pierce, K. M. (Eds.). (1990). *Talking about books: Creating literate communities.* Portsmouth, NH: Heinemann Educational Books.

Slapin, B., & Seale, D. (1992). *Through Indian eyes: The native experience in books for children.* Philadelphia, PA: New Society Publishers.

Sorensen, M., & Lehman, B. (Eds.). (1995). *Teaching with children's books: Paths to literature-based instruction.* Urbana, IL: National Council of Teachers of English.

Stensland, A. L. (1979). *Literature by and about the American Indian: An annotated bibliography.* Urbana, IL: National Council of Teachers of English.

Tway, E. (1989). Dimensions of multicultural literature for children. In M.K. Rudman (Ed.), *Children's literature: Resource for the classroom* (pp. 109–138). Norwood, MA: Christopher-Gordon Publishers, Inc.

Yokota, J. (1994). Books that represent more than one culture. *Language Arts, 71,* 212–219.

Yokota, J. (1993). Issues in selecting multicultural children's literature. Language Arts, 70, 156–167.

Author Index

A
Ackerman, Karen, 17–18
Adoff, Arnold, 39
Adler, David, 25–26
Altman, Susan, 39
Angelou, Maya, 46
Applebee, A. N., 2
Armstrong, Jennifer, 10
Avi, 51–52

B
Baillie, Allan, 18
Baylor, Byrd, 39–40
Bealer, Alex W., 26
Berry, James, 18
Boyd, Candy Dawson, 52
Brooks, Gwendolyn, 47
Brown, Dee, 26
Bruchac, Joseph, 40, 47–48
Burgess, Barbara Hood, 52

C
Carlson, Lori M., 40–41
Catlett, Elizabeth, 44
Chana, Leonard F., 40
Childress, Alice, 8
Choi, Sook Nyui, 19
Clifton, Lucille, 8, 46, 47
Coerr, Eleanor, 60
Cole, Joanna, 48
Conlon-McKenna, Marita, 11, 19
Cooper, Floyd, 47

Cox, Clinton, 26–27
Crews, Donald, 8
Cummings, Pat, 8
Cumpian, Carlos, 41

D
De Trevino, Elizabeth Borton, 11
Dillon, Leo, 8
Dorris, Michael, 52–53, 57
Drucker, Malka, 31–32

F
Feelings, Tom, 8
Fenner, Carol, 11–12
Ferris, Jeri, 32
Filipovic, Zlata, 32
Fleischman, Paul, 12
Ford, M. T., 8
Fox, Paula, 57
Freedman, Russell, 27, 33

G
George, Chief Dan, 41
George, Jean Craighead, 57–58
Giovanni, Nikki, 47
Greenfield, Eloise, 8, 41–42, 46, 47
Guy, Rosa, 8

H
Halperin, Michael, 31–32
Hamilton, Virginia, 12–13, 46, 48–49, 53, 58–59
Hanson, Joyce, 19–20

Haskins, Jim, 35–36, 44
Hautzig, Esther, 33
Hesse, Karen, 20
Hill, Kirkpatrick, 59
Hilts, Len, 34
Hirschfelder, Arlene, 42
Ho, Minfong, 20–21
Houston, James, 13, 34
Houston, Jeanne Wakatsuki, 34
Hughes, Langston, 42–43, 46, 47

I

Izuki, Steven, 43

J

Johnson, J. Rosamond, 44
Johnson, James Waldon, 44
Johnson, L., 5
Johnston, Norma, 27
Joseph, Lynn, 44

K

Katz, William Loren, 27–28
Keehn, Sally M., 61
Kroeber, Theodora, 34–35

L

Lai, Him Mark, 28
Larrick, N., 7
Lechner, Susan, 39
Lester, Julius, 8, 28–29
Levine, Ellen, 29
Levitin, Sonia, 21
Lim, Genny, 28
London, Jonathan, 40
Lord, Bette Bao, 21
Louie, Ai-Ling, 7
Lowry, Lois, 61

M

Mathis, Sharon Bell, 7, 54
McKissack, Frederick, 29–30, 35
McKissack, Patricia, 29–30, 35, 49
McLain, Gary, 49
Mead, Alice, 59
Medearis, Angela Shelf, 44–45
Mohr, Nicholasa, 8, 13–14
Moser, Barry, 49
Myers, Walter Dean, 7, 30, 45, 54

N

Naidoo, Beverly, 14
Namioka, Lensey, 54–55
Nye, Naomi Shihab, 45

P

Palacios, Argentina, 35
Parks, Rosa, 35–36
Pelz, Ruth, 36
Pettit, Jayne, 36
Phelps, Ethel Johnston, 49–50
Pinkney, Brian, 43
Pinkney, Jerry, 8
Porter, Connie, 14
Price, Joan, 15

R

Rafinesque, Constantine Samuel, 48
Rudolph, Wilma, 46

S

Salisbury, Graham, 61
Singer, Beverly R., 42
Smith, S., 5
Smucker, Barbara, 22
Sneve, Virginia Driving Hawk, 7, 45
Soto, Gary, 15–16, 46
Spinelli, Jerry, 62
Stanley, Jerry, 30–31
Steptoe, John, 8
Strickland, Dorothy, 46–47
Strickland, Michael R., 46–47

T

Taylor, Mildred D., 7, 63–64
Thomas, Joyce Carol, 47
Thomasma, Kenneth, 16
Turcotte, Mark, 47

U

Uchida, Yoshiko, 36–37

V

Ventura, Cynthia L., 40–41

W

Walker, Margaret, 46
Watkins, Yoko Kawashima, 37
Whelan, Gloria, 16–17, 22–23

Y

Yarbrough, Camille, 55–56
Yates, Elizabeth, 37–38
Yep, Laurence, 8, 17, 23–24, 38–39, 50, 56
Yokota, J., 5, 8
Yolen, June, 50
Yung, Judy, 28

Subject Index

A

African Americans, 6, 7, 8, 10, 11–13, 14, 19, 22, 26–27, 28–30, 35, 35–36, 38, 39, 41–42, 42–43, 44, 44–45, 46–47, 48, 49, 52, 53–54, 55–56, 57, 58, 59, 62–64
American Revolution, 30, 61
Amish, 4
Apache, 26
Appalachians, 4
Arapahoe, 49
Asian Americans, 28, 43; *see also specific group names*
Athabascan, 59

B

Biography, 11, 31–39, 60
Bosnians, 32
Bull Run, 12

C

Cambodians, 18, 21
Caribbean, 18, 28, 44, 53
Cherokee, 26
Cheyenne, 26
Chinese Americans, 17, 21, 23–24, 28, 38–39, 50, 54–55, 56
Civil Rights Movement, 7, 8, 29
Civil War, 12, 27, 29, 30
Comanche, 33, 34
Council for Interracial Books for Children, 7–8

D

Delaware, 61

E

Euro-Americans, 4, 5, 6, 10, 12, 15, 16, 17, 26, 27, 30–31, 34, 47, 51–51, 53, 54, 55, 57, 58, 61, 62, 63, 64
  as immigrants, 27, 28; *see also* Irish; Jews
  as publishers, 8
  resistance by, 85
  writing about people of color, 7, 32, 88

F

Fiction
  contemporary realistic, 11, 12–14, 15, 16, 18, 19, 21, 22, 52, 53–56, 57–58, 62
  historical, 10, 11, 12, 14, 15, 16–17, 18, 19–20, 21–22, 23, 51, 52–53
  survival, 59
Folklore, 47–50

G

Great Famine, 11

H

Hispanic Americans, 6, 28, 35, 40–41; see also Mexican Americans; Puerto Ricans
History (works of), 25–31
Holocaust, 17–18, 21, 25, 31–32, 33, 36, 43, 61
Hopi, 15

I

Inuit (Eskimo), 13, 58
Irish, 11, 19, 28

J

Jamaicans, 18
Japanese, 60
Japanese Americans, 6, 34, 36–37, 61–62
Jews, 4, 5, 17–18, 20, 21, 25, 31–32, 33, 36, 39, 43, 61
Journals, 66, 71, 81, 85, 89

K

Kiowa, 33
Koreans, 19, 37
Korean War, 19

L

Literature of diversity
 challenges of, 85
 in curriculum, 2–3, 5, 65–85
 definition of, 4–5
 history of, for children, 7–8
 selecting, 87–92
 and self-esteem, 4, 89, 91

M

Mexican Americans, 6, 15–16, 46
Mexicans, 11

N

Native Americans, 6, 13, 15, 16–17, 26, 28, 32, 33, 34, 39–40, 41, 42, 44, 45, 47–48, 49, 52–53, 57, 58, 59, 61; see also individual tribal names
Navajo, 15, 26, 42
Nez Perce, 33

O

Ojibway, 47

Omaha, 32

P

Poetry, 28, 39–40, 41–45, 46–47, 77
Potawatomi, 17
Prejudice, 2, 4, 5, 14, 28, 34, 62–64, 85, 88
Puerto Ricans, 13, 41

R

Reading
 aloud, by teacher, 76, 77
 and drama, 72–74, 77–78, 81
 individualized, 65–74
 and literature circles, 65, 79–85
 silent sustained (SSR), 66
 by student partners, 76–77, 79
 and visual arts, 69–70
 and writing, 71, 77–78

S

Seminole, 44–45
Short stories, 40–41, 46, 49
Shoshone, 33
Sioux, 16, 26, 33
Slavery, 10, 18, 20, 22, 28, 30, 35, 38, 49
South Africans, 14

T

Teacher, role of, 74, 79, 84–85
Thematic units, 51, 65, 74–79, 91
Trail of Tears, 26

U

Underground Railroad, 12, 14, 22

V

Vietnamese, 22–23

W

Winnebago, 16
Women, 27, 28, 35, 49–50
World War II, 7, 33, 34, 37, 60, 62; see also Holocaust

Y

Yahi, 34

About the Author

Julia Candace Corliss teaches at The Mirman School in Los Angeles, California. The recipient of numerous teaching awards, her current research and interest areas focus on areas such as teachers as readers, children's literature, and multicultural education.